CREATING YOUR OWN MARKETING

MAKES GOOD $ AND SENSE

IRA S. KALB

K&A PRESS • Los Angeles

3rd Edition, 4th Printing
Creating Your Own Marketing Makes Good $ and Sense
Ira S. Kalb

Library of Congress Catalog Card Number: 89-83566

ISBN 0-924050-01-2

To my family, friends, students, and clients.

To all those who understand the importance of marketing.

To my customers, the purchasers of this book. Thank you and congratulations.

About the author

Ira Kalb is President of *Kalb & Associates,* an international consulting and training firm which specializes in marketing, sales, management and business systems, *K&A Press,* a publishing firm which publishes books and articles written by Kalb & Associates consultants and affiliates, and *Out-of-This-World Marketing,* a firm which creates ads, brochures, Web sites, and other marketing collateral for clients. He also teaches courses in marketing, sales, management, entrepreneurship, and business systems for major universities and organizations around the world.

Prior to founding Kalb & Associates, he served eight years as Vice-President of Marketing and President of Compal Computer Systems, a California corporation partially owned by Xerox, which specialized in manufacturing and marketing business computer systems and software. As a result of his duties with Compal, Mr. Kalb gained experience in all of the aspects of running a company in a very competitive industry. These duties included: marketing, sales, management, training, operations, finance, accounting, and vendor negotiations. In the performance of his sales duties, he was personally involved in the sales of many hundreds of computer systems and software packages to large and small businesses in a variety of industries.

Before joining Compal, Mr. Kalb spent six years as a staff and senior consultant with such top consulting firms as *Andersen Consulting* and *Economics Research Associates.* This experience has given him an in-depth background in systems, management, and feasibility consulting as well as a staff perspective of companies in many different industries.

He has written, as well as been featured and quoted in, numerous published articles, and is considered one of the pioneers of the multi-billion dollar microcomputer industry. He has appeared on award-winning TV programs, and is the author of the following books from K&A Press: *High-tech Marketing: A Practical Approach, Creating Your Own Marketing Makes Good $ and Sense, Selling High-tech Products, Structuring Your Business For Success, Marketing Your Legal Services, Nuts & Bolts Marketing, A Systematic Approach to Professional Selling, Zero-Budget Marketing,* and *The Fundamentals of High-Technology Marketing: What Marketers Need to Know.*

Mr. Kalb holds a Masters degree in Business Administration and a Bachelor of Science degree in Engineering from UCLA. He was elected President of the UCLA Graduate School of Management Students Association for the 1972 academic year. During that year, he received the American Marketing Association's award as Outstanding Marketing Student at UCLA. He was subsequently elected President of the Southern California Chapter of the American Marketing Association.

During high school and college, he partially supported himself by playing saxophone and other woodwind instruments in various musical groups. Music and art continue to be his major hobbies, with many of his original paintings adorning the walls of his home and office. He has served on the Board of Directors of the Jazz Bakery, a world-renown nonprofit organization dedicated to perpetuating what many consider to be America's only original art form.

Table of Contents

PREFACE • ABOUT THIS BOOK

This book is designed as a practical text to guide marketers and students of marketing through the creation of their own marketing pieces. As with most books on the subject, it provides techniques, concepts, do's and dont's, and actual examples. Unlike most texts, however, it shows how the creation of marketing relates (or should relate) to *universal* marketing structures and concepts.

Too often "how to" books on marketing and advertising focus almost exclusively on the creation of specific marketing examples. As a result, readers are given examples to follow rather than structures and concepts from which they can build their own unique marketing. This tends to perpetuate "me too" marketing rather than stimulate unique marketing ideas. As you'll learn in this book, the key to success in marketing is not only to position your company's products but also to *position each marketing piece* that you create so that it is unique and "stands out" from the crowd.

Certain conventions are used throughout this book. They are explained below so that you understand why certain choices were made in the writing of this book.

The word "Marketing" is used where many others would use "Advertising". This is quite deliberate. Too many people believe marketing is synonymous with advertising and sales. This kind of thinking is not only incorrect, it rarely produces good results. For advertising and other forms of promotion to succeed, they have to consciously consider all the other ingredients in the marketing mix. They have to tie in with the company's Marketing Plan and communicate important messages about the company's product, its position in the marketplace, the places where prospects can buy it, its price, and the company's image. In other words, this book uses the word "marketing" because the items being created really do (or should do) a lot more for the company than advertising. They should prompt prospective buyers to take a buying action that leads to the sale of the product and to a positive image of the company. To do this properly, they should also consider the marketing planning and strategies that have come before and the results and actions that come after.

Throughout this text, the word *Product* is used to refer to both tangible products and less-tangible services. Therefore, readers who are in service industries should know that the book is also written for them when it uses the word "product". There are many good reasons for this. Service is a form of product, and it helps to think of service as a product since it makes it more tangible. Also it's easier to read and write "products" in place of "products and services" when the term has to be used hundreds of times in the text.

This book is written in a more conversational, advertising-type style. As such, many cliches and colloquial words and phrases appear in quotes throughout. There are two "schools of thought" as to where to put the quotation marks. I follow the one that puts quote marks outside punctuation marks when a person is being quoted but inside when they are placed around a play on words or colloquial word/phrase.

While it is correct English to use he, his and him to refer to a person irrespective of gender, many female friends and colleagues of mine don't accept this convention. Because of my sensitivities to their feelings and my recognition that women make up greater than 50% of most consuming markets, I use he/she, his/her, him/her throughout this text. In most cases, you'll notice that I try to avoid this issue altogether by using plural forms such as they, their and them.

Original artwork could not be found for many of the examples used in this book. For this and several other technical reasons, the quality of many of the reproductions are not ideal, and don't do the orignals justice.

I use examples in this book from former and present companies with which I am closely involved. While one might suspect ulterior motives for this, I use these examples for the following reasons:

1. It requires too much "red tape" and takes too long to get legal releases from many of the other companies whose examples I might have used in this book. The time pressures for writing and publishing the book don't allow me the luxury of waiting; and the "sue-crazy" nature of business in America causes me to forego proceeding without having written permission.

2. I really believe the examples I use are good examples and are illustrative of the points I want to make.

3. I am familiar with the thinking and stories behind the creation many of the examples used in this book. This familiarity allows me to enhance the explanations given.

4. I believe the book has more impact if readers can see evidence that I "practice what I preach".

Continuing with this "practice what I preach" concept, the master copy of this book has been produced using a desktop publishing system based on an *Apple Macintosh computer*, a *Hewlett-Packard Scanjet+ scanner* with *DeskScan and DeskPaint* software, *Microsoft Word* word processing program, and *Aldus Pagemaker* page design program.

This book has been written for you so I hope it meets with your approval, and I hope you benefit from this book. If you do, please write me a letter and let me know how it has helped you. Thanks again for selecting this book.

Chapter 1 • INTRODUCTION

"It's about saving money while improving effectiveness..."

Marketing costs are skyrocketing. Irrespective of inflation rates, ever-increasing costs of materials, exploding labor costs, and competition for limited premium media space combine to create this situation.

Since effective marketing is so essential to the health and well-being of an organization, cutting the marketing budget is not the answer. Whatever the costs, good marketing pays for itself many times over. The answer is to do more of the marketing yourself. That is, rather than turn everything over to an expensive ad agency or graphics design firm, you should learn how to create your own marketing pieces, or at least do a lot of the basic conceptualization and copy writing yourself. You can then turn the projects over to outside specialists to put on the finishing touches. In this way, you only pay for expensive outsiders to do either (1) what you can't do or (2) what they do best.

The purpose of this is book is to help you do more marketing yourself so that you can be more self-reliant and more effective without increasing your marketing budget.

Even if you choose not to create your own marketing materials, this book will provide you with much of the information you need to better understand and control the marketing projects which you subcontract to others.

In addition to being educational, I hope you find it to be interesting, fun to read, and useful to your business and personal life.

Notes

Chapter 2 • GOOD AND BAD

"Good marketing pays many dividends. Bad marketing takes money out of everyone's pocket."

As with most other disciplines, there are basically two kinds of marketing — good and bad. Unfortunately, bad marketing is not the exclusive domain of marketing novices. Each year, billions of dollars are thrown "down the drain" for marketing produced by "professionals" as well as non-professionals. What makes this situation intolerable is that professionals (and some non-professionals) charge professional rates for their services. The result is that the organization for which the marketing is produced loses on many fronts. It loses untold potential sales from the ineffective marketing. It loses its considerable investment in producing the marketing (again professionals don't work for free). It loses the cost of placing the marketing in various media (ad rates are not cheap). It suffers image damage from sponsoring poor marketing (consumers don't have good opinions of companies who produce ineffective ads or "cheap looking" brochures). And it incurs very large "opportunity costs" which are the returns that could have been realized if the money thrown away on bad marketing could have been invested in good marketing, product improvements, wage incentives and/or some other productive channels. Considering all these costs — both tangible and intangible, the billions thrown away on bad marketing really amount to a higher multiple of these billions.

The ramifications of bad marketing go far beyond the well-being of the individual organization. Consumers pay for bad marketing by paying higher prices for less innovative products (companies have to recoup their lost investment to survive, and they do it by raising prices and not investing in new product development). The economy often suffers since many consumers switch to lower-priced and more innovative products offered by foreign competitors. Employees pay for bad marketing by receiving smaller wages and benefits. Managers pay for bad marketing via reduced or lost benefits bonuses. All workers pay in the form of lost promotions (the company is not able to expand as rapidly to allow for new positions). Everyone pays a second time in the form of higher taxes to offset the shortfall resulting from smaller incomes. The aggregate effect of people getting smaller wages, paying higher prices, more taxes, and switching to foreign products is a net outflow of money from the country, a growing negative balance of payments problem, and an ultimate reduction in our standard of living.

All this from bad marketing? Believe it or not, it's true. Of course there are many other contributory factors and problems which make matters even worse, but those are left to educators, politicians and many others to solve. The purpose of this book is to help you to produce good marketing — not to solve the problems of the world. At least, not for now.

Whether you are interested in actually creating all your own marketing pieces from start to finish, creating some of the simpler marketing and leaving the more sophisticated projects for your ad agency, participating in the production of marketing pieces, or merely understanding the process so you can better supervise the work produced by outside sources, this book will help you. Practically speaking, most marketers don't have all the tools, talents, or the time to create all of their own marketing from conceptualization to production of the final product. Therefore, in most cases, "creating your own marketing" means that you will produce those pieces for which you do have the tools, time and talents — for example... press releases, news letters, seminar invitations, product description sheets, price lists, manuals, and standard letters, and you will participate in the production of more sophisticated marketing projects, such as camera ready artwork and final printing of ads and bro-chures. You will most likely prefer to "rough out" the text and the layout and then turn the project over to competent ad agencies, graphics design houses, and printers for final review and production. They have the talents, tools, time and know-how to do the kind of job that will make the proper impression on your customers, prospects and other important publics.

However, by doing most of the basic work for them, you can save a lot of time and money, and have better control over the finished project.

If your organization is producing high-tech products and services which are either confidential or difficult for outsiders to comprehend, it is important for you to know how to create effective ad and brochure copy since you are often in a better position to truly understand the product and how to communicate its benefits to prospective buyers. Once the basic concept and copy are created, you will most likely turn the project over to graphics design specialists and printers for final layout and printing.

If you don't have the time or interest in producing your own marketing pieces, this book will at least enable you to better understand and critique the marketing produced for you so that you can perform a necessary quality control function and help insure that good marketing is produced for your organization.

Since understanding the marketing process and how it relates to producing marketing materials is a necessary prerequisite for doing good marketing, a brief review of this process is presented in the following chapter.

Notes.

Chapter 3 • MARKETING REVIEW

"You need a solid foundation, to build anything of value..."

WHAT IS MARKETING?

Marketing is the process by which products and services are developed and brought to market. The process starts by doing *market research* and finding buyer needs in the marketplace that are not being satisfied. These unsatisfied needs are also called market *"niches."* They represent "spaces" or "holes" in the market that are opportunities for companies or organizations to fill. Successful companies uniquely *position* themselves to penetrate these open windows of opportunity by developing *products* and other marketing strategies to satisfy the unfulfilled needs identified. Once developed, the products are *priced* to fit the budgets of market targets, cover costs, make a reasonable profit, provide adequate margins for distributors, and be compatible with the position selected. They are *placed*, or *distributed*, in the marketplace through channels that are convenient and economical for buyers. Once all of the above strategies are in place, the products are *promoted* to inform prospects about the benefits, unique features, availability, and places where they can buy them with the objective of prompting a buying action. A *marketing information system* is developed to collect valuable marketplace information and perform on-going market research to measure the success of these strategies and make necessary adjustments to improve performance.

MARKET PLAN AND CYCLE.

The above process works best when a *Market Plan* is developed to serve as a blueprint for achieving the organization's marketing goals. After introducing the company and its products, the Market Plan identifies market needs, or niches, and determines the potential market for products to fill them. It then describes the company's operational environment giving consideration to the competition, the company's resources and any other factors that might limit the company's ability to realize full penetration of its potential market. Based on these "limiting factors" and the potential, the expected penetration is determined for each of its products. These penetration figures become the key goals for the duration of the plan. The Market Plan then delineates strategies for achieving these goals. These strategies should be based upon "the *5 P's of Marketing*" (Position, Product, Price, Place, and Promotion), the organization's *Corporate Image*, and a *Marketing Information System* to collect information from the marketplace, measure the effectiveness of the organization's marketing efforts, and take necessary corrective action. Since these seven strategies provide the basic foundation of any marketing piece, they are called the *seven building blocks* of marketing.

Since most of the information regarding the product and the other strategies are communicated to the marketplace via promotional strategies. The actual marketing pieces which are developed to execute these strategies become an extremely important part of the marketing effort. To better understand them, it is useful to review and understand the marketing objectives on which they should focus.

MARKETING OBJECTIVES.

1. **Prompt a buying action.** One of the most important objectives of marketing is to prompt sales and/or buying actions. Buying actions include such activities as: Buying the product; Going to see the product; Calling on the phone for information about the product; Sending in a coupon to get more information; Going to a seminar to find out more about the product.

2. **Spark interest.** This involves exactly what it says. The ultimate objective is to generate sufficient interest to get the prospect to buy. However, getting the company name and product into the customer's mind in a favorable position is a good first step.

3. **Provide positive information.** The marketplace needs to be informed about the product and the company before interest or buying actions can be prompted.

4. **Educate.** For high-tech or intangible products, such as services, the market often needs to be educated about the product and company before it can make any buying decisions. Intangibles should be made tangible wherever possible to facilitate understanding.

5. **Get the prospect's attention.** With the more than 20,000 ad messages prospects are bombarded with each week, marketing pieces can make progress if they "cut through" the information jungle and get the prospect's attention.

6. **Get prospects to remember.** In addition to cutting through and getting into their minds, marketing materials should focus on staying there. "Going in one ear and out the other" will do no good. The idea is to "plant seeds" in their minds that, when the time is right, will grow into sales.

7. **Differentiate company's products from the competition.** An effective way to get into the prospect's mind and stay there is to differentiate the company's products from those of the competition. This differentiation is a type of positioning, or fitting into one of the niches (empty spaces). This involves communicating what's positively unique about the company and its products.

8. **Project a favorable image.** Buyers are more likely to be interested in products from companies with which they are comfortable. A positive image is a good foundation for creating this comfortable feeling on the part of prospects.

9. **Build a positive relationship with publics.** Prospects, customers, and other publics are comfortable with products from companies with which they have a positive relationship. Beyond the foundation provided by a good image, marketing should seek to build a personal relationship between publics and the company, its products, and employees.

10. **Communicate with various publics**. While marketing should focus on providing information to prospects and customers, it must also be aimed at the company's various publics including: employees, past employees, prospective employees, vendors, past vendors, prospective vendors, walk-ins, present and future distributors, and prospects who didn't buy. These publics should be viewed as potential unpaid sales people who are ambassadors of good will for the company. If they are impressed with the company and if they are treated well, they can do tremendous good for the company. If treated poorly, they can do untold damage.

11. **Generate New Ideas**. A parallel objective of marketing should be to always solicit new ideas that can turn into successful products. Many new ideas come from a company's various publics. Positively communicating the company's interest in ideas and having mechanisms for recording and referring them to the proper decision makers in the company is an important function of marketing.

12. **Pull customers through distribution channels**. If products are sold through various kinds of distributors, a main objective of marketing should be to prompt buying actions via these distributors, or pull customers "through the turnstiles".

13. **Create customer satisfaction**. The ultimate goal of marketing after making the sale is customer satisfaction. Marketing needs to focus on making the customer happy and keeping the customer happy. Customers are the best unpaid salespeople a company has. If they are happy, they will refer "lots more" business. If they are not, they can cause considerable damage.

Keep these objectives in mind. Understand them. Refer to them often. They can help you "stay on the track" even after you hit the inevitable bumps you'll find along the road.

With this very brief review of marketing, you should be "up to speed" and ready to begin learning how to create effective marketing pieces for your organization.

Chapter 4 • THE UNIVERSAL MARKETING STRUCTURE™

"Marketing pieces will collapse without the proper structure..."

STRUCTURE OF GOOD MARKETING PIECES.

All good marketing pieces do what they are designed to do — sell something. While this "something" is usually the product, it can also be the image of the company or an intermediate step in the sales cycle. As discussed in the previous Chapter, before marketing can really sell, it has to "cut through" the information jungle, grab the prospect's attention, and stay in his/her mind. Will we ever forget *"Mr. Clean"*, *"... squeeze the Charmin"*, *"... the White tornado"*, *"Ford has a better idea..."*, or *"At Avis, we try harder...?* Whether we like these phrases, or not, they have succeeded in "cutting through" congested information pathways; staying in our minds; and helping to sell products for their companies. For the few messages you remember, just think of how many thousands you don't remember. Think of all the money that has been wasted on the ones that never even penetrated your mind. It's in the billions of dollars! These are billions that could have been much better spent on new product development, acquiring and keeping good people, and more effective marketing. Don't waste your or your company's money. Learn how to do effective marketing.

What do the marketing pieces which you remember have in common? What is it about them that has "cut through" and carved a position in your mind? While there are many different answers, good marketing typically follows a formula which I choose to call the *Universal Marketing Structure™ (UMS™)*. Whether you are writing an ad, a brochure, a mailer, a press release, a letter, a magazine article, a newspaper story, a speech, an ad jingle, or whatever, most good marketing follows this structure. An outline of the UMS appears below.

UNIVERSAL MARKETING STRUCTURE OUTLINE.

Good marketing pieces have one or more of the following:

1. **Headline.** This either contains the most important message of the piece or leads to the most important message.

2. **Body.** This section usually supports the main points introduced in the headline. It provides more detailed supporting information usually in the form of product features and benefits and/or variations on the other marketing variables (position, price, place to buy, and promotion).

3. **Close.** The close, as its name implies, is the last thought that is left with the reader within the main text of the ad. Since the main message of a good marketing piece is usually contained in the headline, a good close should *reinforce* and *tie-in* with the headline. The objective is to get the audience to remember the main message introduced in the headline. It should also *solicit a buying action* by asking the prospect to call, write, send in a coupon (if it has one), or buy now to take advantage of a special offer. To measure the effectiveness of the ad or piece, it should contain a code or other market-information-system mechanism.

4. **Picture or Graphic.** The picture is designed to reinforce the important points introduced in the headline and body text. The picture typically shows the product in its best light, attracts the prospect, makes the product more tangible, and serves as a size reference. It is critical that the picture support and be in harmony with everything else in the piece. For example, if the words in the headline and body communicate "a quality product", the picture (and the product in the picture) should have a quality look.

5. **Format or Layout.** The format, or layout, of the piece should be designed to facilitate communication of its most important points in the most concise manner possible. It should allow the busy or lazy prospect to understand the basic message and most important points without having to read the entire piece.

6. **Signature.** As its name implies, the signature of the piece is where companies identify that the piece is coming from them. It always includes the company logo, and often includes a slogan, which is a hook the company uses to stamp its intended position or image in the mind's of prospects.

7. **Intangibles.** To produce the *magic* of great marketing, creativity, uniqueness, and other difficult-to-measure intangibles should be incorporated in each promotional piece.

Because understanding of each of these sections of the Universal Marketing Structure (UMS), is important to creating effective marketing pieces, they will be discussed below in considerably more detail.

THE HEADLINE.

The part of the structure that "cuts through", grabs the prospect's attention, and/or penetrates the prospect's mind is called the "headline". The headline usually has a "hook" which contains the most important message of the piece or leads the reader to the most important message. While the "hook" is usually part of the headline, it can sometimes be an intriguing picture that is used in conjunction with the headline. If the piece is a TV or radio commercial, the hook may be contained in a musical jingle which is designed to stay in the prospect's mind long after the commercial has concluded.

In most cases, the headline will be read or heard by more prospects than any other part of the piece. In fact, studies show that five times as many prospects will read, see, or hear and remember the headline than the other parts of the piece. Many people will browse through publications and brochures or switch TV and radio channels. They don't have the interest or the time to read, view or listen to an entire piece. However, more often than not, they will read or listen to the headline. If it is effective (i.e. if it has a good hook), they will remember it. If they are in the market for the product, it should prompt a *buying action.* Even if they are not, a headline with a good hook is likely to stay in their memory banks until they are in the market for that product. That is why the headline should contain the most important point of the piece, or it should have such a strong hook that it "catches and pulls" the reader into reading and remembering the most important point(s).

Weather writing a newspaper or magazine article, an ad, a brochure, a press release, a product description, a newsletter, a personal letter, a seminar presentation, or any other marketing piece, you should put most of your thought and effort into creating the best headline possible. To assist you in creating effective headlines, the common characteristics of good headlines are summarized below. Good headlines are:

Simple — The best headlines are easy to read and understand. Readers or listeners should easily comprehend them without giving them too much thought.

Concise — The main message should be presented in as few words as possible. To cut through the information jungle and grab the attention of the audience, it has to be as brief as possible. It has to be sharply focused. The main thought of the headline can become unfocused if too many unnecessary words are used.

Alluring — As already mentioned, a strong hook will both grab attention and stay in people's minds. The stronger or more alluring the hook, the better.

Obvious — The main message of the headline should be obvious, unless of course, the headline is just an intriguing hook which leads you to the main message.

Truthful — One of the main objectives of marketing is to build trust and develop positive and long-lasting relationships with buyers. Telling the truth will do this. Lying or exaggerating will not. What's more, even if you are truthful, making statements that give the impression you are stretching the truth will do just as much damage as a real lie. Therefore, you should never use unproven superlatives (such as best, greatest, fastest, largest, and most incredible) in a marketing piece. Use of superlatives without substantiation will only cause mistrust and suspicion. This, in turn, loses sales and causes image damage. Superlatives can and should be used if proof is provided in the piece or is common knowledge. For example, *"Winner of 5 Academy Awards Including Best Picture..."* (common knowledge), and *"CalPRIG Survey Finds Lucky's Prices Lowest Overall for Third Year..."* (proof provided) are good examples of headlines which use superlatives with proper proof.

Focused on market targets — Headlines that identify their targets are the most effective. Prospective buyers reading, viewing or listening to the piece say to themselves, "This is for me." If they know it is for them, they take notice, they listen more attentively, and they are more inclined to take the next step. Novice marketers think that if they focus on specific targets, they will be eliminating potential buyers. However, what really happens is that their message becomes so diluted that primary targets don't notice and others don't have a strong enough interest to take notice. Focusing on market targets is an important part of positioning strategy. You can focus or use positioning in the headline in a variety of different ways. You can appeal to (1) A particular industry ("Lawyers Give Expert Testimony on Compal Computers" or "Here's what writers who write for a living write about Compal), (2) A particular job level ("Today's managers are expected to learn word processing in their spare time... Fortunately, that's all it takes"), (3) People who need a particular type of product to solve a problem, ("Finally. A portable FAX...), (4) A customer type ("IBM is making it their business to answer questions about yours"), (5) Buyers sharing common characteristics ("The most unforgettable women in the world wear Revlon"), and (6) Prospects wanting to know how you are different from the competition ("We try harder"). The above list merely provides some examples. You should understand that the number of possible target groupings is virtually limitless. The main point is that people viewing or hearing the headline should know that you are talking to them.

If the headline is fashioned properly, it should flow easily and naturally into the body text or other parts of the marketing piece.

THE BODY.

The body of the marketing piece performs the following functions:

Provides detail to support the headline and explain its main message — This detail is often presented in the form of features and benefits of the product. Good marketing mentions unique features, but concentrates on the benefits of these features to the buyer. For example, the phrase "this computer can accommodate up to 16 megabytes of RAM" discusses the feature "16 megabytes of RAM". If this feature is mentioned in the body of the piece, it should be accompanied by an associated benefit such as, "this is enough capacity to run all the most advanced software with plenty of room for expansion as your needs grow." Features describe the product, often in terms which are too technical and dry. Benefits sell the product. They sell target audiences on what the product features will do for them.

Answers Objections — As those involved in sales know, to be successful selling a product, you have to answer the prospect's objections to the product and company. Good marketing pieces will acknowledge and answer common objections. Normally this is done in the body of the ad. For example in a Harris/3M copier ad, the piece addresses an objection of many copier users — misfeeds. It does this in the body of the ad by explaining that, "Each is designed with a straight paper path to help prevent misfeeds." The product feature "straight paper path" was used to answer the "misfeeds" objection with the benefit "...to help prevent misfeeds."

Concentrates on the Benefits of Unique Features — The text of the body should concentrate on the benefits of those features which are unique to the product and the company. Rather than concentrate, the body of most pieces contains too many extraneous thoughts and words. In such cases, the main points become lost in a lot of unnecessary verbiage. Since the body of a piece has a tendency to be too long anyway, you should follow this simple rule: *"When in doubt, cut it out."*

Builds on the Interest Generated by the Headline — It's important that the body of the piece hold the media reader's interest. There is always the danger of a big "let down" if the body does not measure up to the headline. It should at least "live up" to the promise of the headline. Really good pieces build on the interest generated by the headline with cleverly focused and well-written copy.

Tells the truth — As with the headline, superlatives such as we're number one, our product is the best, fastest, biggest, easiest to use, and least expensive should be avoided unless proof is provided. The most convincing proof is provided by well-respected, independent industry authorities. Why should unproven superlatives be avoided? Target audiences don't believe them. They hear them so often that they "tune them out" or ignore them. Moreover, they mistrust anyone who uses unsubstantiated superlatives. This mistrust, in turn, adversely affects sales as well as the image of the product and company.

Well-written body text will flow naturally into the close of the piece.

CLOSE.

The close of a marketing piece is almost as important as the headline because it is the last main thought that is left with the reader, viewer or listener. Assuming that the headline contains the main message of the piece, the close should *tie-in* with the headline to *reinforce* its message.

After *tying-in* and *reinforcing* the main points, it should *solicit a buying action*. That is, it should ask prospects to call, write, send in a coupon, stop in, or buy the product by a certain date to take advantage of a special offer. Marketing pieces that don't solicit action waste advertising dollars. If you don't ask for a date, you usually won't get one. If you don't propose marriage, you are not likely to get married. And, as good sales people know, if you don't ask for the order, you won't get many orders. It's that simple. Therefore, at the end of all marketing pieces ask the audience to take the next step, or *buying action*.

After soliciting a buying action, the close should perform another important function — provide a mechanism for measuring the effectiveness of the marketing piece. For example, a print ad may include a response coupon. This coupon should contain an *MIS code* which tells marketers the exact publication, issue, and page from which it came when is returned by the prospect. In this way, it can help you to determine what publications are the most effective source of leads. In the next marketing budget, resources can be reallocated to those which are most effective, or "pull" the best. Other popular forms of *MIS codes* include: a *special extension* on an 800-number, a bar code on a coupon or warranty card, or a specific name which the prospect is instructed to mention when they call or visit. Finally, the close should psychologically *conclude the ad.* It does not have to be the last physical section of the ad — the Signature usually is —but it should wrap up the main theme.

PICTURE OR GRAPHIC.

It's an old cliche, but it's true — *"A picture is worth a thousand words."* A good picture or graphic that is well coordinated with the headline and the body of the piece will reinforce the main message and sometimes communicate this message better than any words ever could.

There are times when a picture should be used, and when it shouldn't be used. It should be used if...

1. The product or subject of the picture is good looking and/ or makes a positive impression on the target audience. If people are used in the pictures, they should be trained models. Trained models know how to pose in front of cameras to reinforce the message of the piece. People-on-the-street and company employees usually do not.

2. It helps to build a positive relationship between the company and the target audience. Celebrities are frequently used in ads and brochures for this purpose. Buyers "know" them and are comfortable with them. Their association with the company and its products serve as an

endorsement which quickens the building of a relation-ship between the prospect and the company. It is a similar situation to the one in which you are introduced to someone by a friend whom you know and trust.

3. It reinforces the main message of the piece. It should not introduce a completely different message.

4. It works in accordance with the marketing strategies employed in the piece. For example, if the piece talks about a high-end, quality product, everything in the picture should communicate quality. If the piece talks about a compact, fit-anywhere product, the picture should communicate this message.

5. It is believable. Unless the picture is an obvious carica-ture which uses humor or a futuristic theme as a hook, it should be believable.

6. It can be easily understood. Sometimes difficult-to-un-derstand pictures serve as hooks to interest readers. However, unless the target audience is comprised largely of puzzle-loving intellectuals, the images should be very easy for target audiences to quickly understand.

It shouldn't be used if...

1. The product or subject is ugly and there is no comic intent. If the product is unattractive, there are basically three choices: (1) Don't use a picture; (2) Distort the picture (using camera angles, multiple images, screens and/or filters) to make it intentionally funny, (3) Use line drawings or graphic images of the product/subject in place of an actual photo.

2. It will reveal trade secrets. If a picture will reveal sensi-tive information to competitors or foreign governments, it should be avoided. While this may seem obvious, you'd be surprised how many times this mistake has been (and continues to be) made.

3. The cost of reproduction is prohibitive and/or will not appreciably affect the expected response. Many four-color pictures are very expensive to reproduce in ads and brochures. Unless, they will yield a justifiably higher

return on your investment, it makes no sense to use them.

4. The picture does not successfully communicate the main message of the piece. This can be easily tested by asking a representative sample of the target audience to reveal the thoughts that come to their minds when they see the picture.

5. It detracts, rather than adds, to the piece. Pictures that are not in synch or harmony with the headline and body will detract from the effectiveness of the piece much the same way as waves that are out of phase are subtractive rather than additive.

FORMAT or LAYOUT.

The layout of the piece refers to several different issues including: how the elements are arranged on the page; how they line up relative to each other; what colors are chosen for the background, foreground and type; what typefaces are selected; what point sizes are selected for the different sections of the piece. Whatever format elements are selected, the *layout should enable prospects — especially those who are busy or lazy — to easily and quickly pick out main points of the piece.* To do this effectively, the following recommendations are offered:

The layout should be clean and uncluttered — Too much text squeezed into too small of a space communicates only negatives about the company and its products. Since it looks disorganized, it communicates a lack of organization. Because everything is cramped into one small space, it gives the reader the impression that the company is "cheap" or doesn't have the money to "do it right". It also gives the impression that the company is unsophisticated. Prospects are often afraid to buy from unsophisticated companies since they believe they'll deliver inferior products or they'll go out of business and consequently not be available to take care of the products they've sold.

It should use highlighted sub-headlines — If the text of the piece is longer than just a few small paragraphs, it should have highlighted sub-headlines (usually boldfaced, underlined, indented, or italicized). This gives the busy reader the option of quickly scanning the main points in the sub-headlines or, if interested, reading the entire piece. It communicates to prospects that the company does not want to waste their valuable time.

It should be fun and/or interesting to read — Too many marketing pieces are boring. As discussed in the section on the body of the piece, cleverly-written text can help. However, well-written text can be buried in a poor layout, and unexciting text can be made significantly more interesting with proper formatting and design. Proper formatting communicates sophistication and know-how. Its attractiveness also generates reader interest.

The layout should be logical — In most Western cultures, text is read from top to bottom and left to right. Recognizing this, the format of the piece should usually put the headline at the top, followed by the picture or graphic, the body, and the close (which may or may not have a return coupon). Marketing pieces which require the reader to scan the piece in haphazard fashion should be avoided. They only cause the reader to miss important information and to become frustrated. The last item of the piece should be the company logo or slogan. There also may be trademark or disclaimer notices at the very bottom in very small print.

The type face should fit the message and the image — For example, if a company is seeking to position itself as an innovative leader of quality high-tech products, it should use a high-tech type face which exudes state-of-the-art professionalism. Unsophisticated marketers use too many different type faces in the same piece. This communicates clutter and confusion, and does not look aesthetically pleasing. One, two, or perhaps a maximum of three should be used. Unless used for a special effect or to highlight sub-headlines, multiple typefaces should be avoided.

Colors should be correctly utilized — As with type faces, colors should be selected to support the message of the piece and the image of the company. High-tech companies will want to use *PMS (Pantone Matching System)* colors that communicate high-tech innovation and precision (grays, blues, cool reds, blacks and whites). Companies selling plants and pottery may want to use warm Earth tones. Using Earth tones in a marketing piece for a high-tech company might cause dissonance and confuse the prospect. The colors used in the ad should not clash with the colors used in the logo. If the piece is going to be viewed by market targets in foreign countries, the various meanings of colors should be understood and considered. For example, in Malaysia, green is associated with illness and death. In China, red is a lucky color; whereas in nearby Thailand, yellow is considered lucky.

Point sizes should be properly selected — As with typefaces, you should not use too many different points sizes in the same piece. Novice marketers make this mistake too often. This communicates confusion and disorganization. Size changes should be used to indicate changes in hierarchy or type of text. For example, headlines, sub-headlines, body text, picture captions, disclaimers and trademark notices may all have different point sizes.

In addition to holding the number of different point sizes to a minimum, the sizes selected should be chosen with care. Too frequently, novice marketers select point sizes which are too large. They do this because they think bigger is better. Using type which is too big is the *visual equivalent of shouting*. It usually does not achieve the desired result. Instead, it often has one or two negative effects. Firstly, there is the psychological effect where the audience thinks the company is insecure and has to compensate with large type. Secondly, there is the *"front row of movie theater"* effect (FRMT) whereby the reader has to hold the piece far away just to read the text. This is similar to the action taken by most movie goers who prefer to move toward the back of the theater to see the movie in better perspective. Too many ads — especially those in newspapers — make this mistake that is important to emphasize here.

SIGNATURE.

As with the signature of a letter, the signature section of any piece should be the last item on the page or the TV screen, or in the case of radio, the last words of the radio spot. In addition to identifying that the piece comes from your company, the signature serves several other purposes. Graphically, it helps to visually frame the piece and define the bottom border. If a slogan is used in conjunction with the logo, it stamps the company's image or position in the minds of prospects. It serves to signal the *final end* of the piece (the only items that typically appear after the signature are trademark identifications and disclaimers in very small print).

As already discussed, items are typically read left to right and top to bottom. Therefore, the best location for the signature is usually the bottom right of the piece.

The marketer should assume that anything placed after the signature has a low probability of being read or heard. Even so, you will find pieces which place second and third slogans and other text after the signature section. This is amateurish, confusing, and should not be done.

THE INTANGIBLES.

The structure described above presents a tangible formula for you to follow. The idea is that anybody who really understands the UMS and the marketing prerequisites can create competent marketing. To create, really successful marketing, however, something more is required. The intangibles... the "things" that are difficult to teach someone else how to do... they can turn competent marketing pieces into great marketing. The two most important are good taste and creativity/uniqueness.

Good Taste

Some people have it. Some don't. You might ask, how can this be taught to someone who does not? While it's not easy, it can be done. The problem arises when people think they have good taste when they really don't. For them to be successful in marketing, they have to acquire good taste. As with all marketing, step one is to find out what others think. You can ask close friends if they think you have good taste. Many may not tell you to avoid hurting your feelings. Better yet, without telling them that you created it, ask them to tell you if a marketing piece you designed exhibits good taste. If possible, ask people in your target market. Also try to ask graphic designers, architects, and art directors of successful ad agencies since they are typically the best choices for opinions. Step two is to start scanning print media which is considered to be the epitome of good taste. For men's clothes, it may be *GQ or Esquire* magazines. For women, perhaps it is *Elle* or *Cosmopolitan.* For ads, it is one of the Advertising publications such as *Adweek* or *Ad Age.* Regularly scan these magazines and ask yourself why the design elements you see are considered to be examples of good taste. Remember, the idea in effective marketing is to please others — particularly your target prospects — not just yourself or your boss.

Creativity/Uniqueness

As with good taste, creativity is something that is difficult (but not impossible) to teach to someone else. Everyone has a creative ability. It's part of everyone's persona. In some, it is buried more deeply than in others. As we grow up, most of us learn how to "fit in" with everyone else in society. Some of us are even taught that creative people are "weird" and are to be avoided. As a result, to avoid being thought of as unusual or abnormal, we bury our creative abilities. The first step in re-awakening our creativity is to believe that you have it. The next is to experiment by selecting examples of marketing pieces and by changing them slightly to make them more unique. Making something unique will help you to develop creativity and vice versa. Remember, you want your marketing to stand out and not blend in with the crowd. To do this, you have to overcome your compulsion to be "blend in with the crowd". Try it. You'll be surprised how this new way of thinking can really work for you.

In addition to good taste and creativity/uniqueness, there is another important intangible concept that is interwoven with the UMS of successful marketing pieces. It's what I call the non-linearity of time and space. This concept is so important that it deserves it's own section.

NON-LINEARITY OF SPACE AND TIME.

In his Theory of Relativity, Einstein postulated that distance and time change at speeds approaching the speed of light. On Earth, there is an analogy to this theory. When you're having a good time and you're feeling good, time seems to go very fast. On the other hand, when you are miserable or you feel sick, time seems to go slowly and sometimes even stand still. You should think of this non-linearity of time when creating marketing pieces. Even if they are lengthy, effective ads, brochures, seminars, etc. are enjoyable and "go by" very fast. Those that are not seem to take forever. This means that you can't just measure the length of an ad or its headline by the number of words. You can't say that it's too long merely as a result of its physical length. You also have to take into consideration its psychological length. The same is true of space. Ineffective ads seem cluttered even if they have a lot of physical space separating elements whereas effective ads seem to have sufficient space even if the elements are placed very close together. This is the non-linearity of time and space. You should remember it when you are creating marketing pieces. The idea is not to measure lengths and spaces in only physical terms, but to also consider the psychological aspects. The marketing piece should be so informative and enjoyable to read, view or hear that it will seem to be go by too quickly. Readers, viewers and listeners will be left wanting more. This "wanting more" will cause them to take some sort of buying action that will eventually lead to a sale of the product.

EXAMPLE.

To facilitate your understanding of the UMS presented above, it is useful to look at the structure of an actual marketing piece to see how it follows the considerations discussed above.

Figure 4-1 shows an ad that was placed in the *Los Angeles Times* by a local electric company, *Southern California Edison.* The purpose of this ad is to instruct home and apartment owners how to save money on their electric bill during the winter. Energy companies will often provide this advice in an effort to help avoid angry customer reactions to higher bills, minimize the possibility of outages during peak demand periods, and improve their image.

Headline: "How to win the cold war." This headline uses a play on words to "hook" the reader's interest. The "cold war" usually refers to relations between Western allies and Soviet Bloc countries. In this case, it refers to fighting the cold temperatures during the winter. Since the "cold war" is a term with which most readers are familiar, the play on words is even more effective. The familiar term is likely to be more easily understood and remembered. The primary target audience is homeowners, with a secondary audience being anyone who has to pay his/her own utilities. Used in combination with a clever picture, it is clear and easy to understand the main message of this ad.

Body: The body of the ad flows easily from the headline picking up the "fighting the cold weather" theme. It offers suggestions to help consumers save money on their winter electric bills — a good use of both the Price and Product marketing variables. It is well-written and easy to read.

Close: The close reinforces the headline with its closing comment "With a little help, you'll win the cold war hands down." It also supports the idea of saving money as described in the body of the ad by telling consumers they will "save on (their) energy bill all winter long". It solicits action by asking readers to call for a free booklet (good uses of the Promotion and Price marketing variables). In this solicitation, it cleverly describes some of the money-saving suggestions provided in the booklet.

AD EXAMPLE

How to win the cold war.

It's time to take up arms. Just follow these simple suggestions and you can defend your energy bill against high heating costs this winter.

Use energy wisely and save on your winter bill.

You can start saving simply by using your trusty caulking gun to weatherstrip and seal cracks and gaps around your windows.

You can also install attic and duct insulation. It can reduce your energy use for heating as much as 40 percent.

Better yet, you can install a new high-efficiency electric central heat pump in place of your existing system.

You'll save on your energy bill all winter long. Call 1-800-952-5062 for your free booklet.

For more ways you can combat high energy costs, call us for your free booklet, Hot Tips for a Warm Winter.

You'll find all you need to help keep your heating bills down this winter. Like the latest energy-efficient improvements for your home. And tips on how to keep cozy without using a lot of heat.

Or talk to one of our representatives about more ways you can save.

With a little help, you'll win the cold war hands down.

Together we can brighten the future.

Southern California Edison

Figure 4-1

Picture: The main picture is part of the hook. It's intriguing because it's a comical caricature of a man dressed in winter garb carrying a caulking gun like a weapon to "fight the cold war". This picture is well-done. It ties in with the main message of the headline and directly with one of the suggestions in the body. Notice how the model or actor is able to use a comical expression to reinforce the ad's message. An employee or "man on the street" is not likely to be as effective. There is another small picture of a tightly-closed window in the close section. It is strategically located next to the reference to the free booklet. It is a picture of the cover of the free booklet which is entitled "Hot Tips for a Warm Winter". In addition to reinforcing the main points of the ad and helping to "sell" the free booklet, it serves to make the ad visually more interesting and to break up the longest paragraph so it looks more inviting to read.

Layout/Format: The layout of this ad is excellent. It begins with an easy to read headline and is logically laid out from top to bottom and left to right. Each sub-headline of the body is highlighted with slightly larger boldfaced type. Busy readers can merely read the main headline and the two sub-headlines to get the main points of the ad. Each suggestion or main point under the sub-headlines is highlighted by new indented paragraphs which are kept short so they are easy read.

All pictures are strategically located near the points to which they refer (the main picture relating to both the headline and the paragraph that discusses caulking windows and the secondary picture referring to the free booklet). Both pictures break up the text in a graphically pleasing way.

The selection of basically one type face for the text of the ad shows good taste and graphic integrity. As with most marketing pieces, the type faces of the slogan and the logo are different from that of the body text. The headline and sub-headlines are merely boldfaced versions of the same type face.

Point size variations are made with discretion. Changes are only made for the headline and sub-headlines as well as the closing slogan and logo.

Signature: The company's slogan ("Together we can brighten the future") and logo are discreetly placed at the bottom where they belong. They belong there because they serve to give a finality to the ad, help to frame the ad graphically, and act as the company's signature. It tells readers "this ad comes from us."

Overall, this is a very good ad. It starts with a very effective headline and does not lose the momentum generated by the headline. Since most utilities have a monopoly in a given geographical area, their marketing typically focuses on selling service (in this case helpful suggestions) and image. They want consumers to look favorably upon them so they receive on-time payment of bills, minimal complaints when brownouts occur or service is interrupted, and little or no opposition for rate increases.

Hopefully, this example has served to further your understanding of the Universal Marketing Structure. Along with the previous explanation of the UMS, it should serve as a useful guide for you to follow when you create marketing pieces for your organization.

While the very best marketing pieces are structurally strong throughout, the important point to remember is that the headline is usually the most important since it is the part of the piece that is most likely to be read and remembered. Therefore, particular care and attention should be devoted to creating excellent memorable headlines.

Since the key to writing effective headlines is creating good hooks, the following Chapter will be devoted to providing you with some suggestions for creating these hooks.

Notes.

Chapter 5 • CREATING EFFECTIVE HOOKS

"They should grab people hook, line and sinker..."

THE MARKETPLACE IS FLOODED.

Wherever you go, the marketplace is drowning in a sea of marketing messages. Advertising is everywhere. It's in the traditional places such as magazines, newspapers, retail establishments, industry directories, phone directories, brochures, billboards, mailings, television, radio, movie theaters, bus benches, buses and taxicabs. In recent years, it has begun to turn up in such non-traditional places as bus shelters, fax machines, computer billboards, faces of airline tickets, and videos. In addition to the ever-increasing number of channels for these marketing messages, there an escalating number of companies and organizations who know that they have to advertise to compete.

THE NUMBERS ARE STAGGERING!

There are over 1,500 companies listed on the New York Stock Exchange and more than 5 million other corporations in America. There are more than 14 million small businesses in the U.S. and an ever-growing number of foreign companies marketing their products in the United States. In order to sell their products, these millions of companies are having to do more marketing than ever before. In their book Positioning: The Battle for Your Mind, Al Ries and Jack Trout explain that "With only 6% of the world's population, America consumes 57% of the world's advertising." Jay Chiat, co-founder of the highly-acclaimed Chiat/Day ad agency, estimates that, with all this advertising, the average American is exposed to 20,000 advertising messages per week!

That's a lot of advertising. It boggles the mind. In fact, minds are so boggled and overloaded that they "tune out" most of these messages just so they can properly function. How do you get through to all those minds that are already so cluttered with information? Jay Chiat calls it "crashing through the rubble." Others call it cutting through the information jungle, or finding a space or window in the prospect's mind. Whatever you call it, you have to use creativity and ingenuity to as never before. You have to create headlines with strong hooks that reach out and grab people. They have to distinguish your company and products from the ever-growing crowd. They have to be unique and different. They have to wake up audiences who have fallen asleep as a reaction to being overexposed to too many marketing messages which say basically the same thing.

To penetrate the clutter, the late Rosser Reeves, former head of the Ted Bates Ad Agency, developed the concept of the *Unique Selling Proposition*. The idea of the *USP* is to have each and every marketing piece make a proposition to the customer that the competition cannot or does not offer and to have this "uniqueness hook" be so strong that it can pull new customers to buy the product.

EASIER SAID THAN DONE.

It's easy to say that headlines need to have strong hooks. It's much more difficult to create them. That's why marketing professionals who are successful at creating good hooks are typically paid a lot of money. Whatever they are paid, they are worth it because their creations stand out, grab attention, and generate buying actions.

What many marketers don't realize, however, is that they don't always have to turn to highly-paid professionals to generate effective headlines. They too can create them. It takes some know-how, practice, and confidence. This book can help with the know-how, and by giving you a technique to follow, it can give you some confidence. You have to supply the practice and work on the confidence (which should come from a combination of practice and the right attitude). The right attitude comes from believing that you can do it. You can. You just have to believe it.

TECHNIQUES

There is technique to creating hooks. It's not all creative genius from marketing prodigies. A good place to start is to examine some of the techniques used to create them. They include:

Humor. Everyone likes to laugh and be entertained. People are attracted to humor. Therefore, humor helps to build a relationship between the organization and its target audience.

Play on words. Using a play on words, pun, or phrase with multiple meanings attracts interest. It causes readers to stop and take notice. Also, if done properly it can make the company look clever and sophisticated.

Suspense. Suspense draws interest. People can't wait to find out how something intriguing will be resolved.

Turning an intangible into a tangible and vice versa. Since intangibles are often more difficult to understand, making them tangible facilitates understanding. If this is done in a clever way, it can be a powerful hook since people like to learn and comprehend without realizing they are learning. Tangibles can be very boring and difficult to distinguish from the competition. In order to add interest, excitement, and psychological value which will allow the company and its products to stand out above the competition, intangibles such as success, happiness, youth, status, sexual fantasy, and sophistication are incorporated. Headlines for perfume, jeans, deodorant, and cars often use such hooks.

Metaphors. Good metaphors are like clever analogies. If prospects knows and understand the analogy, they can better comprehend the main message. New-found understanding can be a powerful hook.

Answering objections (about the product, company, or industry). An important part of the selling process is answering objections. When all objections are answered, prospects buy. People are hooked by having their answers resolved in a way that makes them feel comfortable about buying.

Jargon of market targets. Buyers focus on messages that are speaking directly to them. By using their unique language or jargon, they take notice because they know you are talking specifically to them.

Cleverness. Most people appreciate cleverness. It takes them away from the boring, ordinary, mundane, "me too" kind of messages that occupy most of their time. It wakes them up from their "tuned out" stupor.

"What's wrong with this picture". This often involves deliberately misspelling a word, turning the ad upside down, leaving out a word, or using other gimmicks to grab attention. Again, people take notice just because it is different and not so boring. They want to find a solution.

Cliché. Clichés can be effective hooks because people already understand what they mean. Using them in a new context of selling a product can be clever and/or humorous.

Riddle or Question. A riddle or question builds suspense. It hooks readers because they want to find out how it is resolved. Moreover, the resolution is usually clever and humorous.

Ironic Twist. Irony, or the use of words to convey the opposite of their literal meaning, can be a very effective attention grabber. It makes the headline more interesting. It's clever. It helps people to remember.

Clarity and Simplicity. Some headlines that present a clear and simple message use the clarity and simplicity as a hook to "cut through" and stand out from the crowd. After all, many people appreciate the straightforward approach, and few if any object. Sometimes the quickest path into the brain is a straight line.

Free and Discount. Free and discount are powerful marketing words. They hook people. Even though many are skeptical about such offers, when they are legitimate and properly communicated, they work.

Deadline. Just as with the words free or discount, the use of a deadline to save money or take advantage of a special offer is a powerful hook to get prospects to buy.

With these various techniques in mind, let's look at some actual headlines and examine the kinds of hooks they use to "crash through the rubble".

HEADLINES WITH GOOD HOOKS.

"What was tedious and expensive is now just expensive"

This headline is used to sell a new technology-based service that saves a lot of time and effort in creating television commercials. The headline uses a humorous twist as a hook. Nobody expects the advertiser to say that the service offered is expensive. That's what makes it funny. While the hourly rate of this new service may be high, prospects know that the time and effort saved will more than compensate for the expenditure. The headline communicates this without saying it. Therefore, in addition to making the point in a humorous way, the headline scores more points with its audience by coming off as being honest in an understated way (an essential step in developing a relationship with the prospects and customers).

"All Harris/3M copiers are delivered with a component that can't be broken... (The reader must now turn the page). Our Promise."

This headline uses several "hook" techniques. The first is a riddle which creates suspense since the reader must turn the page to find out what it is that can't be broken. It uses the ironic twist technique since the reader knows that hardware components can be broken. Probably the most interesting technique is that it makes the intangible "promise" tangible by referring to it as a "component".

"Write from the start"

This headline uses the play on words technique. It is selling a word processing program called *Write.* The word "Write" as used has several different meanings: (1) the name of the program, (2) the verb "to write" as in what you do with a pencil or word processor, and (3) a pun for the word "right" (since "right from the start" is a well-known cliché). "From the start" also has multiple meanings. As part of the cliché, it means beginning. In the case of the verb, it implies the word processor is very easy to learn and use since you can "write" or use it right away after you purchase it. In this way, the headline also uses the "answering objections" hook since it answers an objection many prospects have — the fear that new computer software will take many hours to learn.

"Lawyers give expert testimony on Compal Computers"

Lawyers reading this ad know that the ad is talking to them. In addition to using the word "Lawyers", it uses the legal jargon "expert testimony". Since this headline is from a testimonial ad, the word "testimony" takes on a double meaning which makes it even more clever.

"Here's what writers who write for a living write about Compal"

This headline is also from a testimonial ad. It uses a clever juxtaposition and repetition of words to identify the target market — serious writers who write for a living.

"How old is young?"

This headline is used to sell advertising in Youth Beat magazine for the American Youth Market. It's objective is to hook advertisers who want to reach the 18 to 34 audience since the magazine claims 63% of its readership falls into this category. The question (or riddle) format, the irony inherent in the question, and the clarity and simplicity of the words act together as a strong hook to pull readers into the body of the copy.

"Bad Ads Free"

This is a headline used by an ad agency to promote their services. It uses a combination of techniques. The most obvious is the word "Free". "Bad Ads" also generate interest since most people want to find out why someone would advertise "Bad Ads". This headline also uses the irony and double meaning hooks. The ad firm is communicating that they are so confident in their work that the prospect doesn't have to pay if they are unhappy with the agency's work. The irony is that bad ads really aren't free. They end up costing more than good ads (insertion costs, lost sales, opportunity costs etc.).

The above examples are hooks which stand on their own. That is, most people can get a good understanding of the message without looking at an accompanying picture or reading associated body text. They were presented above without the remainder of their ads for that reason. It is important to understand, however, that many excellent marketing pieces use the headline together with the picture and/or body text as the hook. In these cases, the headline's can't stand alone. While these dependent hooks are very effective, it's always better to design hooks that can stand alone. The reasons include: more people will read them and absorb the message (something can happen to the text or the picture and busy readers may not have time to read or comprehend them); and stand alone hooks can be used on various marketing pieces, such as mailers, that may not have room for pictures or text copy.

PRACTICE MAKES PERFECT.

Looking at lots of headlines, analyzing why they are good or bad, saving the good ones in a file, and copying the styles in your own marketing will help you to create good hooks.

After you go through the above process, you should practice creating your own. You should write down as many as you can think of in a pad or notebook. Even if you don't plan to use them, you should keep them on file. You never know when they might come in handy. If you create any masterpieces, you should consider having them copyrighted or trademarked. Perhaps you can use them as slogans. While you are deciding, you can always put a ™ as a superscript following the headline, and be sure to establish your date of first use (get it notarized, or send it to yourself and keep it in the *postmarked* envelope). This should protect you until it you officially register it — with an®.

Since *pride of authorship* is a "disease" from which most of us suffer, you should test your headlines on colleagues, prospects and customers. Don't give them just one and ask for their opinion. They might be obligated to say nice things because they know you created it. Give them a list and ask them which they like the best. Make sure you listen to the criticisms. After all, they are the ones you have to sell. You're already sold.

Now that you have some guidelines for putting hooks in your headlines and for creating marketing pieces that follow the UMS, it is useful to explore how these techniques fit into the process of creating marketing pieces from start to finish. The next Chapter will discuss the various steps involved in this process.

PRACTICE EXERCISES.

1. Find two recent magazines that are routinely read by prospects in your target markets.

2. Copy or tear out two ads with headlines that you feel have good hooks and two that don't.

3. Explain why you feel they are good or not so good.

4. Re-write the weak ones.

5. Write a good headline to promote your products in one of the above magazines.

Chapter 6 • THE CREATION CYCLE

"It often takes more than six days and six nights..."

WHAT IS THE CREATION CYCLE?

The Creation Cycle is the sequence of steps involved in the process of creating effective marketing pieces for the organization. Depending on the media selected, they can vary somewhat. In most cases, however, these steps include the following:

1. **Review and understand the Marketing Plan.** Anyone who is selected to create a marketing piece for an organization should make sure that he/she understands the company's business, the goals of the marketing plan, and the strategies to achieve these goals. This includes understanding how customers and prospects view the product and the company. If there is no Marketing Plan, one should be developed. In its absence, creators of marketing pieces should do some research to thoroughly understand the product from the company's and, more importantly, from the prospect's point of view. This research does not have to be time-consuming or expensive. It can be accomplished by talking with customers, prospects, and people in the company who have daily conversations with customers and prospects (i.e. sales, support, training, and service people).

2. **Review the promotion strategies in detail.** Since most marketing pieces are part of the promotion strategies of the Marketing Plan, these strategies should be reviewed and understood in detail. The marketer should insure that the piece he/she is about to create will "fit in" and be coordinated with all of the other promotion strategies as well as the pieces in circulation and under development. Too many companies make the mistake of having one marketing piece conflict with another. This only causes problems — not the least of which is confu-

sion on the part of prospective buyers. Confusion causes buyers to postpone or withdraw intended purchases and to look to the competition to fill their needs.

3. **Review the positioning strategies in detail.** The marketer who creates the piece must understand the positioning of the product and company before getting started. The piece that is created must reinforce rather than conflict with the intended positioning. Unfortunately, too many creators of marketing pieces don't fully understand the importance of staying within positioning boundaries. A mistake too often made is positioning a company or product as being top-quality, but designing marketing pieces which don't communicate this message and don't have a quality look. If the promotional piece doesn't exude quality in all its aspects, many prospects will question the quality of the product and the company, and will postpone their purchase decisions. The image or position communicated by the marketing piece must be in harmony with the other marketing variables used in the piece. That is, if a quality position is selected, the product represented in the promotion piece must have a quality look, any price reference must reflect the notion of quality, and the place(s) where company products are distributed must have quality images. The important point to remember about positioning is that it has to be approached from the audience's point of view. It has to strike a chord in the minds of prospective buyers. It has to appeal to their needs and tastes. Many either forget or don't understand this. They create marketing which appeals to company insiders — not to the audience.

4. **Create and outline the concept of the piece.** Rough out the headline, body, close, picture or graphic (if appropriate), and layout. Again, you should put most of your time into creating a headline with a strong hook. If the piece is going to be a TV commercial, rough out a story board (which is a sequence of dialogue and pictures, much like a cartoon in the Sunday newspaper). If you have a desktop publishing system, use it. If not, do it the old way — with "exacto" knife and tape. When

doing this, always keep in mind the main objective of the piece — to sell the product and/or create a buying action.

5. **Get a consensus from the decision makers.** If there is no consensus, start over — unless, of course, you believe so strongly in your ideas that you are willing to fight for them. If you adopt this latter course, make sure you have proof, such as audience data, to back you up. Otherwise, you will be accused of such sins as "pride of authorship" and a lack of objectivity. If there is a consensus, proceed with the next step making any necessary changes agreed upon in your meeting with the other decision makers.

6. **Finalize the headline and the copy.** Revise and edit your words until you have them just right. Have trusted "objective eyes" review and approve the piece before submitting it to decision makers for final review and approval. To avoid problems later, it's a good idea to have the decision makers "sign off", or approve in writing, the final text copy.

7. **Select the media.** Different magazines have different space and mechanical requirements (page, column and screen sizes). The final layout of the piece is going to depend on which publication is selected. Similarly, different television networks may have different requirements (although there are more standards in television than in print media).

For Print Media

8. **Finalize the layout and the graphics.** Create what's called a "dummy" or a mock-up of the final piece. This serves two main purposes. The first is to give the decision makers a good idea as to how the final piece will look. The second is to serve as a guide for the printer. From the dummy, the printer can obtain necessary information about size, color, number of pages, folds, number of photos, etc. and can estimate the price of the job. Upon creating the dummy and getting price estimates and approvals, schedule any photo sessions or

graphic design work. Make sure the people working on the photos, art and the graphic design review and understand the concept, headline, and copy of the piece. The more they know about it, the better job they will do. It should be noted that "dummies" can vary from being very crude (but actual size) replicas of text, photos and art to almost finished copies. The sophistication of the dummy really depends on the discretion of the designer and the decision maker(s). In this sequence of steps, it is assumed that the dummy is a crude mock up in which headlines and photos are hand-drawn, the actual words of text are provided on accompanying typewritten sheets, and the size and location of text is indicated by hand-drawn lines.

9. **Finalize the Type.** Specify the typeface (Helvetica, Futura, Garamond, etc.) the size (point size), orientation (up and down or italic) horizontal spacing (character pitch), spacing between lines (leading), and weight (thin, medium, bold). These decisions are based on positioning (in the marketing sense), aesthetic, and technical considerations. That is, the type has to be consistent with the positioning strategy of the product; it has to look good; and it has to fit within the layout. The process of getting type to fit within the layout is appropriately called copyfitting. The entire process of finalizing type is called typography.

You can select type and do copyfitting yourself. But you will need some simple tools. First, you'll need a type book or spec book which you can get from a local typographer (typesetting company), most large printers, or your ad agency. Next, you'll need a special ruler, or type gauge, called a Haberule.

The first step in copyfitting is counting. That is, you have to count the number of typewritten characters in the body text of your copy. In the old days, this was relatively easy since most typewriters had pica (10 characters to the horizontal inch) or elite (12 characters to the inch) spacing. In more recent times, typewriters and word processors can do fancy tricks with character spacing. Therefore, the most universal method of counting starts with drawing a light pencil line through the approximate location of the right margin. You have done this correctly if the extra width of longer lines balances the extra space of shorter lines (of course if your text is right justified all lines will have the same width except for indented lines and lines which end paragraphs or are part of lists). Count the number of characters (including spaces and punctuation marks in an average line). Multiply this by the number of lines in the copy. Add to this the number of characters to the right of your drawn vertical line. Subtract from this the number of spaces to the left of your drawn line.

The next step is sometimes called casting off. It involves translating the number of characters you have counted into the typeface you have selected. The objective is to have your text printed in the desired typeface and size fit into the space allotted in your layout. Since type is measured in picas (the size of pica type) and points, you will need your Haberule which uses these units of measure. One pica = 1/6 of an inch (or there are six picas to the inch). One point = 1/12 of a pica (or there are 12 points to each pica). Using your Haberule, measure the width of the type block in your layout (your "dummy" mock up) in picas. This is called the measure. Select the typeface and point size you want from your type "spec" book. For this typeface and point size, your type book should have a table which tells you how many such characters will fit in one pica (if there is no such table, you can use your Haberule to determine this number). Multiply this number by the measure (or width of your type block in picas). The result is the number of characters in a line. To determine if the number of lines of this size and style type will vertically fit in your type block, you have to use the trial and error method. That is, you take the number of characters you counted in step one, and you divide this number by the RESULT obtained above. This yields the number of lines. However, it does not allow for spacing between lines, called leading. The leading is measured in points

usually from 1 to 12 and can really change the "depth"
and look of the text. For example if you want 10 point
type (elite size) and you want 2 point leading, you allow
12 points for each line on your Haberule. Multiplied by
the total number of lines, you get the total depth of your
text block. You compare this with the depth allowed on
the layout of your dummy. Using trial and error, you
play around with the point sizes of the letters and the
leading to fit your layout and to achieve the look and
readability you want for your text. While this process
may seem complicated, it really isn't once you do it.
Moreover, its automatic if you have a computer to do it
for you.

Once the type decisions are finalized, the text is typeset.
If you have typesetting or sophisticated desktop publishing equipment, you can do this yourself. If not, you will
have to send your selections to a typographer for final
typesetting. For sophisticated work, you will most likely
want to send your work out to a professional typographer. They usually have a greater variety of typefaces,
sizes, and weights; and they most likely have much
more sophisticated equipment for producing more sophisticated results.

10. **Finalize the photos and the art.** Photos and art are
produced in accordance with the design embodied in the
"dummy". Since the reproduction of photos and art can
be very confusing, we will take it slowly. Firstly, it helps
to understand that mass producing photos and art on
paper requires a different process than developing prints
from film negatives (which is what is done when you get
your own photographs developed). It's different for a
number of reasons. The two most important are: it is
much more expensive to mass produce photos by developing negatives than by printing them using ink on
paper; and using a photographic process for photos and
art would make their integration with printed text on
the same page much more difficult.

Halftones. In order to reproduce photos or any art that
has gradations in tone between black and white (also

known as continuous tone art or halftones), the images must be photographed through a screen which breaks the tones into dots. Darker areas have more dots in the same space and lighter areas have less dots. The same is true for color reproduction, except more screens (up to 4) are used.

Text and line art. Text and line art (art that is black and white with no shades of gray in between) can be photographed directly without any screens since there is no shading to replicate. If you did, the black would have dots so close that there would be no space in between and the white would have no dots at all which is exactly where you were before you used a screen.

In many cases photos and art require some preparation before photostats are made. The following are some of the typical preparation processes that are involved.

Cropping. The art is cropped to indicate areas that are not to be included in the final version. It also indicates the new center of the art or photo.

Enlargements/Reductions. The remaining area to be shown in the final version is often enlarged or reduced to fit the layout. This should be indicated by actual numbers or by percentages (i.e. 3" to 5" or enlarge 67%).

Type of stat. The type of stat desired should be indicated such as, matte or glossy finish, first or second print.

Identification. Each photo and piece of art should be identified with a unique number for reference and tracking (i.e. making sure all original elements are accounted for).

Positive/Negative. For effect, the art and the photos are sometimes reversed where the blacks on the original become the whites, and vice versa. This reversal should be indicated.

Flopping. Sometimes you want to reverse the image so that the right side becomes the left, etc. This is called flopping and should be indicated.

Position Only. If the photostat is to be used for position only on the final mechanical layout, it should be so indicated.

All of these indications should be made in the margin of the photo or the art, or on a transparent plastic or translucent tissue paper sheet affixed to the art. This is sometimes also done on the photo with a grease pencil. However, great care should be used with this type of marking to avoid damage to the original.

A photostat (which is technically a photo print made on paper directly or from a paper negative) is then made. Usually, the photostat will be used for size and position only, but in some cases where high-quality is not required, it is actually used in the piece.

11. **Produce the mechanical.** When the type comes back from typesetting (usually in the form of galley proofs) and photostats are made of the photos and art, they are reviewed for accuracy and quality, and necessary corrections are made. The final typeset copy and line art are created and pasted up on a board according to the desired layout. Spaces are left, in the layout, for photos and halftone art. The end result of this paste up procedure is called the "mechanical". It is also referred to as "camera-ready art" since it is ready for the printer or graphic design house to photograph. The purpose of the mechanical is to (1) integrate all of the type and line art elements of the piece on one board so it can be photographed by the printer, (2) to indicate the exact location and layout of all elements in the piece so they can be correctly assembled on the final film master, and (3) include all instructions to the printer, in printer jargon, so he/she can proceed without requiring your on-site supervision.

12. **Select the printer.** If the piece is an ad to be placed in a newspaper, magazine, or directory, you will not have

control over the printer selected. The publications all use their own. For those pieces over which you do have printing control, select the printer according to your technical needs and your budget, as well as the printer's availability and reputation for service. Technical issues are important since many printers can't do all types of jobs. Some are good at black and white but don't do a good job with color. Others are good with small pieces but don't have the appropriate press for large pieces. Make sure that the printer you select can do a good job of accommodating the following: the number of colors in the piece, the size of the piece, the desired level of quality, and the number of pages to be printed. It's a good idea to shop printers. Ask for samples of similar work, and references for you to call. Make sure that you have alternate printer sources should the one you normally use be unavailable or technically unable to do your job.

13. **Create film master.** If you are running an ad, a graphics house or ad agency may create your film master. Otherwise, the printer will typically do it. Whoever does it will receive the mechanical along with photostats and/or original photos and continuous-tone art. The typeset text and line art (art made from black lines with no shading) are photographed directly from the mechanical. Photos and continuous tone art (art that has shading) are photographed separately because they require different handling. They may have to be cropped and/or blown up or reduced in size to fit the layout; they have to be photographed through a screen which transforms the various tones, or shading, into dot patterns which conform to the screen requirements of the media selected (different magazines and newspapers have different screen requirements); and items to be printed in full color have to be photographed through four different screens positioned at different angles (each representing a shade of red, yellow, blue and black). That's why "4-color" printing is so much more expensive than black and white or two-color printing.

Once the photography of these elements is completed, they are cut and placed (or "stripped") into position on a sheet of plastic (often called a goldenrod) along with the photos previously taken of the mechanical. The final layout of all these elements is arranged in exact accordance with the original mechanical.

It should be mentioned that there is a simpler and less costly method of obtaining a halftone. In this method, a velox is made which translates the continuous tone art elements into line art. The velox is an already-screened photographic print of the original art on paper (rather than film). It can be cut to shape and pasted into position on the mechanical with the other line art so that it can be photographed together. In this way, the steps of separately photographing the continuous tone art and stripping it into place are avoided. The only drawback of this method is that it does not yield as high quality of a reproduction as the other process discussed above. However, for all but the very highest-quality work, it is usually sufficient — especially if the budget is tight.

14. **Obtain approval.** A crude blue or brown print is made of the film master. This "blueline" (or "brownline") is then submitted to the decision makers for final review and approval. Again, it's a good idea to get them to "sign off" their approval. Once approved, notify the printer or publication to proceed.

15. **Finalize the paper selection.** If you have control over the printing, and you haven't already done so, you will need to select your paper stock. Believe it or not, your choice of paper stock can be critical to the success of your marketing piece. It must fit with your chosen position, the color of the ink selected, and with the objectives of the particular piece you are running. Don't skimp on the paper. The few dollars you save will be minuscule compared to the damage to image and sales that your decision might cause. In many cases, you can make up the price differential by buying the higher quality paper yourself. Paper wholesalers will often quote you a better price than the printers will. In any

event, it is a good idea to shop the price and compare it to the amount the printer has quoted you. If you are wondering about the ink, that decision is usually made along with the selection of the type. The specific PMS color of the ink is noted on the overlay that protects the mechanical or on the mechanical itself in non-reproducible blue pencil.

16. **Create printing plate.** Once the final blueline is approved the image on the final film is transferred to a plate by means of a chemical etching process. This plate is then mounted on a printing press. After being inked, paper is fed into the press and, depending on the process used, the ink is transferred either directly onto the paper or first to a rubber roller (offset process) which, in turn, transfers the ink onto the paper.

17. **Do press check.** Send someone to do a quality control check on the first pieces run through the press by the printer (you probably won't be able to do this in the case of ads placed in publications). Make sure this "someone" knows exactly how the piece should look and is good at proof reading and catching printing mistakes (misalignment of lines, unevenness of color, spots, inconsistency of color from copy to copy, etc.). This reviewer should also check any folds to make sure that the paper stock selected is not breaking apart at the folds.

18. **Make any necessary changes.** Don't print the job unless you are satisfied it will look the way you want it to. While you may have a critical deadline and you may have invested a lot of money in the camera-ready master, the costs are small relative to the damage caused by printing a faulty piece.

19. **Have the printer run the job.** Make sure the nth copy is of consistent quality to the first few copies. If there is something wrong, have the printer correct it. Remember, although you're under time deadlines, your image and your sales are at stake so make sure the final product looks good.

Note: For certain print applications such as newsletters, product descriptions, and news releases, many of the above steps can either be eliminated or done automatically using a properly-outfitted desktop publishing system. Type can be selected or created, copyfitting can be completed, photos and art can be scanned into the system, elements can be integrated into a final layout, and the final piece can be printed — all automatically. There are attachments available that can even create camera ready art for ad slicks, 4-color printing, and slides for presentations. These will discussed in more detail in a later Chapter on "Tools". Even if you are using such a system, however, knowledge of the standard mechanical process is beneficial to your final result.

20. **Audit the published piece.** If mistakes were made in the color, the placement, or any other aspect of the piece, make sure you notify the publication, the printer, or other responsible party right away. Follow up to insure that they give you an appropriate amount of credit.

21. **Measure the effectiveness.** Each piece should be coded so that responses can be traced to the specific issue of a particular publication. Such coding greatly improves the quality and reduces the cost of your on-going marketing research into the effectiveness of your marketing. Leads, sales, and other types of buying actions should be measured and traced back to each piece as faithfully as possible. In this way, you can make necessary improvements in future insertions, improve response, and avoid "throwing money down the drain" for ineffective ads.

For TV Media

Pre-production

8. **Create, review and finalize the concept and script.** It's a good idea to test the concept with your various publics (prospects, customers, employees, vendors, etc.) before proceeding. This normally involves showing them

the storyboards at the beginning of the project and the finished commercial at the end. Make sure the script sells the product and enhances the company's image. Avoid anything that would offend any groups. There are too many stories of commercials that have unintentionally offended particular groups of people — particularly women and minorities.

9. **Select models/actors and locations.** Make sure the *looks*, *voices* and *personalities* "fit" with the concept of the piece. For example, "clown-like" characters are not particularly effective selling serious business products (particularly those of financial institutions and office automation companies) whereas actors with "classy" images would not be effective in fast food or household cleaner commercials. If the commercial is going to exclusively use animation, animals, or pictures of the product, the voices of the actors become even more important.

Production

10. **Rehearse and film or video tape commercial.** Make sure you (or your trained representatives) attend the sessions. Make any necessary changes during the filming of the commercial.

Post-Production

11. **Schedule film post-production.** If the commercial is shot on film, film post-production is where the film is edited in nearly final form. You should review and approve the edited film master before proceeding.

12. **Schedule video post-production.** Television broadcasts are made from video tape. Therefore the edited film master has to be transferred to video tape for broadcast. During the transfer process, the color is corrected to cover up any mistakes made in filming and production or to make the commercial look better. After being transferred, any special effects are added (more tricks can be done on video tape than on film) and a final edit on video tape is made. You or one of your

representatives should attend and give input to the transfer and edit sessions.

13. **Review and sign off.** Make sure that the decision makers review and sign off on the final edited video master. This saves a lot of time and trouble later.

14. **Send to TV stations for broadcast in target market areas.** Once approved, copies of the edited master are made and sent to the appropriate TV stations for broadcast. Masters and elements used to make masters are stored in an environmentally-controlled vault for future use.

15. **Audit the broadcast.** You or your representatives should audit the broadcast in all markets to insure that the commercial was not pre-empted by news flashes, technical difficulties, or other interruptions. Since TV time is very expensive, you should make sure that you receive credit for any interruptions.

16. **Measure the effectiveness.** You should have systems in place to measure the effectiveness of your pieces. If you don't, you are just throwing a lot of money down the drain. With the information collected you can make revisions that will make the piece more effective and thereby make and save a lot of money.

For Radio

8. **Write script.** Make sure it fits within the time guidelines of the time you intend to purchase from the radio station. If the script does not quite fit the allotted time, you may not have to change it. The reason is that there are sophisticated audio post-production techniques which can be used to squeeze in more words into less time or spread fewer words over more time without noticeably affecting the sound of the voice.

9. **Select Narrator.** The voice of the narrator is extremely important. You will hear the same voices on different commercials. Make sure that if you are selling a professional office product, you don't use a narrator who is identified with dog food or yogurt commercials. The

narrator's voice has to fit with your positioning and promotional objectives.

10. **Rehearse.** Make sure you are happy with it. The time to make changes is now, not after it is broadcast.

11. **Create tape master.** This usually involves recording the commercial as rehearsed, editing it, and adding special effects for final broadcast.

12. **Send to radio stations for broadcast.** Make copies of the master and send them to the radio stations who are selected to broadcast. Store the master in an environmentally-controlled vault for future use or archiving.

13. **Audit the broadcast.** As with the other media, the broadcast must be audited in all markets to insure the commercial was run in its entirety without technical problems. Make sure you receive credits from commercials that were not broadcast in their entirety.

14. **Measure the effectiveness.** Again, the effectiveness should be measured to improve future broadcasts and to insure that the dollars invested are being productively spent.

DOING IT RIGHT.

Many marketers make life difficult for themselves. They don't always follow a logical sequence of steps when creating a marketing piece for their organization. When this happens, it lengthens the Creation Cycle and sometimes causes more serious problems. One of the most common problems is losing sight of the company's marketing objectives and strategies formulated to achieve them. In order to avoid such problems, marketers should understand that there is a Creation Cycle and that the process will proceed much more smoothly and quickly if the steps are followed in a logical sequence.

During every step of the process, marketers should remember that the objective of the piece is to sell something — usually the product. They should also remember and use good marketing fundamentals. In particular, everything about the piece should focus on the audience's point of view. Their needs, their tastes, their interests, their convenience (i.e. in reading the piece, in calling for information, or in going to a local place to examine the product), their objections, their attitudes, etc. It should tell the truth and not insult their intelligence.

While doing it right is never easy, it's much easier and much less costly than doing it wrong and suffering the consequences of image damage, losing sales and/or having to do it over and over again.

After reviewing the tools you'll need to create your own marketing, the remainder of this book will concentrate on providing you with techniques for doing it right. Because the vast majority of companies and organizations concentrate their marketing efforts on print media, marketing pieces which appear in print will be emphasized. The concepts and principles used in these media, however, carry over to TV, radio, video and other marketing vehicles.

Before going over the techniques required to create print ads, brochures and other marketing pieces, let's review the tools you will need.

SUGGESTED EXERCISES

1. Find an ad in a magazine or newspaper.

2. Identify the company's positioning strategy as indicated by the piece.

3. Circle the word(s) which reinforce this strategy.

4. Think about the steps that the marketer who created the piece followed.

5. Write down those steps on a piece of paper.

Chapter 7 • THE TOOLS OF THE TRADE

"With the proper tools, you can do wonders..."

In recent years, technology has automated virtually every part of the creation cycle. Word processing, desktop publishing and graphics systems have become welcome additions to the marketer's tool chest. The objective of this Chapter is to introduce you to the tools you are likely to need when creating your own marketing.

WORD PROCESSORS.

In the "old days", copywriters created their headlines and copy with pencil and paper. Many graduated to typewriters. While some still use these tools, most use word processors. Word processors are computers with software that enables you to automate the typing and editing process. They allow you to create original text on a TV-like screen, correct this text on the spot or at a later time, and print it out at high speeds while you do something else. Studies show that writers using word processors are typically 300% more efficient than they are using electronic typewriters. This boost in efficiency allows the same results to be achieved in one-third the time of other more manual methods.

As these word processing systems become more sophisticated, they are allowing copywriters to become more and more efficient. In addition to automating the typing and editing process, they are doing the following additional tasks for copy writers: automatic spell checking, word look-ups, thesaurus look-ups, retrieving of famous quotations by subject matter, etc. If they get much more advanced, they will evolve into an *expert system* that does the copywriting for the marketer with little human intervention.

DESKTOP PUBLISHING SYSTEMS.

With the appropriate computer hardware (computer with large internal memory, sufficient permanent storage, graphics capability, high-resolution screen, scanner, and laser printer), marketers can have desktop publishing capability on the same system that they do their word processing. Desktop publishing enables you to take text created on the word processor, integrate it with graphics, create sophisticated page layouts, and print the resultant pages on paper in whatever type styles you choose. With additional compatible equipment, actual photos can be scanned into the system for integration with text and graphics, and the finished page can be either printed or made into a mono or multi-color separation to be later printed by a publication or a professional printer. There are even devices for using a video camera to scan an image directly into the system for immediate integration with a document. In this way, different poses can be stored and tried without waiting for photographs to be developed. Desktop publishing systems are also being hooked up to both overhead and slide projectors for use in conducting seminars and other sales presentations.

With the proper hardware and software, virtually every step in the creation cycle prior to publishing can be duplicated on this system. The *dummy, mechanical,* and *final camera-ready art* can be created. For certain applications the final *ad slick* or printed version of the piece can even be made. However, unless the system has the sophistication of the highest-quality printing and graphics houses, it will not be able to create brochure-quality printing or magazine-quality ad slicks of the quality level that can be produced by these outside houses. As systems become more and more sophisticated and lower and lower cost, such capabilities are likely to become available to most marketers. For now, the equipment is too big and too expensive for *every* marketer to have in his/her own office.

Nevertheless, the desktop publishing systems that are available can do a lot of finished marketing pieces such as newsletters, press releases, invitations, product descriptions and price lists; and can save a lot of time and money in the preparation of more sophisticated pieces for final layout and printing by printers, graphics houses, and ad agencies.

Even if you have these automated systems, you may still want to know about the traditional tools used in the process of creating marketing pieces for an organization. Such knowledge will help you to understand how to better use your automated systems (many of them use traditional terminology) and will give you an appreciation of the time and trouble you are saving by employing your automated solutions. Furthermore, you may still want to use some of the traditional tools for back up and to create mock-ups or dummies of the piece you will ultimately create on your computer. Of course, if you don't have automated systems, you need to know about the tools required to create mechanicals (camera-ready art) the "old-fashioned" way. To cover all cases, the most commonly-used tools are discussed below.

DRAWING SURFACE.

If you are going to create your own mechanicals manually (without a desktop publishing system), you need a drawing surface. In its simplest form, it is literally a wooden board. A more sophisticated version is a table whose height is adjustable and whose drawing surface can be angled from horizontal to almost vertical. It's important that the surface be relatively smooth or a least free from holes and that it have a metal edge (also called a "true edge") built in or clamped to one or both sides (the metal edge should be on the left if you are right-handed and on the right if you are left-handed). The purpose of the metal edge is to accurately guide a T-square to help insure accurate alignment of work. A well-appointed drawing surface typically has a wooden lip at the bottom edge. This prevents tools, artwork, and other loose items on the surface from falling off — particularly when the surfaced is angled from the horizontal. The drawing surface should be big enough to accommodate the size of work you plan to do. For most marketers, this is at least 24" from top to bottom and 30" from left to right with 30" by 42" being more common. Since you may do a lot of cutting on the drawing surface, you should protect it with a large piece of illustration board (the same material used as the basis for the mechanical). You should square this board to the edge of the surface (using a T-square described below) and fasten it in place with masking tape. While there are many good-quality brands of illustration board on the market, Bainbridge #172 and Crescent #200 are commonly used. In addition to protecting the surface, it serves as a sort of underpadding which facilitates drawing inked lines and helping with the traction of your cutting tool.

T-SQUARE.

For those doing mechanicals manually, the T-square is one of the most valuable tools in the tool chest. This tool serves as an edge for horizontal ruling, cutting, and squaring (with the help of a right-angle Triangle). To avoid the smearing of ink, a T-square with a beveled edge is recommended. If you inherit one without such an edge, you can put a narrow piece of masking tape just back from the edge. This will elevate it just enough so it won't smear the ink or allow it to spread underneath. T-squares come in a variety of sizes — the most popular being 20", 24" and 26". Choose the size which will accommodate the largest dimension of the work you plan to do.

TRIANGLES.

Triangles are used in conjunction with T-squares to draw vertical lines and perfect angles. The bottom edge of the triangle is moved along the horizontal top edge of the T-square. While they usually come in clear plastic, they are also available in metal. The plastic ones should not be used as a guide for cutting since they will get nicked and cut and lose their true edge. As with the unbeveled T-square, you should put a narrow piece (1/2" width) of masking tape just back from the edge to avoid smearing and spreading of ink. Triangles come in a variety of angles and sizes. The 45 degree and 30/60 degree triangles in 6" and 12" sizes are the most popular.

RULER.

If you have a choice, you should invest in a ruler which has its units marked off in picas and agates (units of measure used by newspapers so that 14 agate lines equal one inch) as well as inches. Picas will help you to do copyfitting and to give measurements to printers, and agates will assist you in sizing ads for newspapers. The most commonly used sizes are 16 and 18 inches.

In addition to providing units for measuring lengths, rulers are used as an edge for cutting and tearing. A metal ruler is recommended since it is more likely to keep a true edge when used to guide cutting tools than other types of rulers. As with the T-square and triangle, its a good idea to put a piece of masking tape just back from the edge of the ruler to avoid ink from smearing and spreading underneath.

MECHANICAL DRAWING TOOLS.

A set of mechanical drawing tools are necessary for most marketing tool kits. This set usually includes: compasses for drawing circles in pencil or ink, a pair of metal dividers for transferring measurements, and an ink ruling pen which can be adjusted to create lines of varying thickness.

PENS AND PENCILS.

A variety of different pens and pencils should be in every tool kit. In addition to the ruling pen referred to above, you should have ball point pens in blue, red and black ink; felt-tip pens or markers of various colors (which can be used in creating dummies, for marking instructions without making indentations, for color-keying plastic overlays, and for highlighting); a fine-tipped quill or technical pen for making delicate marks and corrections; and lettering pens with interchangeable points for various hand-lettering tasks. As for pencils, you should have a soft No. 2 pencil for sketching; a hard 2H pencil for making thin light pencil lines; a light blue pencil for making non-reproducible guidelines and instructions on a mechanical; a red pencil for flagging corrections and instructions that you want to be seen and/or reproduced; a grease pencil for marking on glossy surfaces that you want to later remove; and a chisel-point soft pencil for making wide, dark pencil marks — often used for generating simulated lines of text on a dummy.

ERASERS.

Since hard erasers can damage and discolor the artwork as well as create unwanted eraser crumbs, soft erasers that can be molded into any shape are most frequently used for erasing most pencil marks. Depending on the materials used in the mechanical, stubborn marks can be removed with certain chemical or hard erasers if they are used with caution.

INKS AND PAINTS.

Black india ink is the most common ink used for drawing. Sometimes blue, red and brown inks are also used. Usually, the inks used are waterproof and they make a permanent, non-erasable line (water-based inks are too susceptible to smearing from the sweat of one's hands). Therefore, to cover mistakes or imperfections in drawn lines, a white opaque gouash, acrylic or poster paint is used. This paint is also used to make white lines on a black background. If a mistake is made applying the white paint, however, it cannot be corrected with black ink since the ink won't penetrate or adhere to the slick painted surface. For this purpose, black poster paint must be used.

CURVES AND TEMPLATES.

For drawing accurate curved lines, you should have several French curves in your tool kit. They come in a variety of sizes and shapes. You should select the ones you need according to the work you need to do — adding new ones as they are required.

Since drawing small circles is difficult with compasses, you should have a circle template in your tool kit. The same is true of ellipses (which are usually used for circles drawn in perspective). Ellipse templates usually range in perspective from 10 to 80 degrees.

CUTTING TOOLS.

Since it is used for cutting paper in creating mechanicals, the most frequently-used cutting tool is the single-edged razor blade. The X-acto knife is probably the most popular form of single-edged razor blade because it comes with a easy-to-hold handle and the blades can be easily replaced and discarded when they become dull. Using this tool, cuts are made by sliding it along the guiding edge of a ruler, T-square, or metal triangle. As mentioned previously, only metal edges should be used for cutting.

For illustration board and other materials heavier than paper, a matte knife (which is a tool similar to the one used to cut open cardboard boxes) is recommended. An X-acto knife or single-edged razor blade will get stuck and lose its sharp edge too easily if used to cut these heavy materials.

To cut circles and ellipses, X-acto knifes are used in conjunction with templates. For larger circles, a cutting tool can be attached to your compass. To cut large curves, a metal French curve can guide a cutting tool or a swivel knife can be used.

TWEEZERS AND ADHESIVES.

Once shapes are cut to the proper size by various cutting tools, they are placed in position on the mechanical by tweezers. The pointed type of tweezers are most frequently used for delicate work. There are always times when you need to correct one character of copy or a single punctuation mark. Pointed tweezers come in very handy for these intricate jobs.

Cut-out pieces are held in place on the mechanical by various adhesives. Rubber cement is the most popular because it is economical and easy to use. You simply apply some rubber cement to the illustration board where the varies pieces of copy, photos, and art are to be attached (the location of these pieces is usually indicated by faintly drawn non-reproducible blue guidelines). You similarly apply rubber cement to the piece you want to attach, and you fix it in place with your tweezers. If you are out of alignment, you merely pick up the piece of paper with your tweezers and re-align it. Rubber cement comes in either regular or spray cans. If large regular cans are used (since it's the most economical way to buy rubber cement), you should also invest in a pint-sized rubber cement dispenser which has a brush applicator attached to the lid. You will also need thinner to thin out rubber cement that has thickened and to un-cement pieces that are fixed in place. You should use a special thinner applicator to avoid spilling or overusing the thinner. These applicators resemble small oil cans. To remove un-wanted dried rubber cement from edges, you can rub it off with your fingers. Since your finger might smear ink or cause other damage, you can also remove it with a ball of other dried rubber cement.

Some large graphics houses and commercial studios use hot wax as an adhesive. While it does an excellent job, the hot wax machine is very costly. Therefore, it only makes sense if you have large volumes of work and you are going to use it all the time.

TAPE.

Additional adhesive products in your tool chest include two types of tape — white masking tape and matte finish cellophane tape. The white masking tape is used for a variety of purposes including: securing illustration board to your drawing surface, securing the illustration board of the mechanical on which you are working, hinging an overlay or protective cover on your mechanical, covering over something on the mechanical that you don't want in your final piece, and putting on the underside of rulers, T-squares and triangles so that ink does not smear or bleed underneath.

Cellophane tape is also used for a variety of purposes — particularly those which require you to be able to clearly see what's underneath. The matte finish is most useful, because you can write on it if you need to.

Both tapes come in a variety of sizes. One-half inch width is the most frequently used.

OVERLAYS.

Overlays are typically used to protect the mechanical, indicate areas of color to be printed on the final piece, and to give instructions to the printer or graphics house. Tissue overlays are often used to protect the mechanical artwork. Often times, another protective cover of darkly-colored construction paper is used over the tissue paper, but not always. Acetate overlays are frequently used to indicate areas of color. Instructions are often written on both tissue and acetate overlays. If you are going to write on acetate overlays, be sure to select appropriate marker pens that allow you to write on this material or to select the type of acetate that allows you to write on it.

MEASUREMENT TOOLS.

In addition to the ruler and dividers discussed above, you should have a couple of special measuring tools in your tool kit. The first is called a Haberule. It is a special ruler which is used to measure how much type of a particular size and style will fit into the type block of your layout. It contains several scales for measuring and converting different point sizes into picas. Recalling a previous discussion in the Chapter on "The Creation Cycle", there are 12 points to the pica and 6 picas to the inch.

Another important measuring tool is the proportional scaling wheel. While there are simple methods to determine new dimensions when art is scaled up (enlarged) or down (reduced), a proportional scaling wheel gives you the new dimensions in seconds. It works on the same principle as a slide rule.

CROPPING DEVICES.

Whether or not you enlarge or reduce the art in your piece, you may want to crop it to eliminate unwanted portions or to emphasize certain features. For this purpose, you should have a cropping device in your tool chest. You can purchase a ready made cropping tool, but it is so easy to make your own that most people use the "homemade" version. It consists of two L-shaped pieces of cardboard that are of equal size. They can be moved relative to each other in such a way that they cut off varying portions of a photo or piece of art. That is pulling the "Ls" apart will show larger portions of the art and pushing them toward each other will reduce the portions shown. When the amount of cropping is just right, crop marks can be made in the margins of the art (or on an overlay) so that the printer or graphic house will only photograph the wanted parts of the art work.

COLOR FORMULA GUIDE.

To select colors of papers and inks, you should have a color formula guide in your tool kit. This guide has examples of virtually all printable colors referenced by number. One such guide is published by Pantone, Inc., 55 Knickerbocker Road, Moonachie, New Jersey 07074. It shows the color, gives the relative amounts of other colors used to make that color (in both parts and percentages), and assigns a reference number.

TYPE BOOK.

Typographers provide type style books of all the type faces or fonts which they have available. You should contact a typographer which you plan to use for your typesetting work to send you their type specifications book.

PAPER SAMPLE BOOKS.

Paper companies provide samples of the paper they make and/ or sell. It's a good idea to keep sample books of the most popular papers. You should have a book for stationery, business card stock, brochure stock, inexpensive internal papers, label stock, envelopes, etc.

TYPE FILE.

You should maintain of file of unique and interesting graphics symbols and lettering that you find in various books and publications. You never know when you might want to use these symbols or special lettering to accent a marketing piece on which you are working. Such letters and graphics are often used for the first letter of text in a marketing piece, book, newsletter, etc. They are also used to accent new paragraphs or highlight important sections of a piece.

PHOTOGRAPHIC EQUIPMENT.

Whether you plan to do your own photography or subcontract this function to outside experts, you might want to keep some basic photographic equipment on hand for a variety of purposes. The most common include: taking pictures for company newsletters, photographing products for product brochures and sales manuals, photographing the executives for annual reports or resumes to be included in proposals, photographing an example of the kind of photo you want to use for an ad (which you will later have done by an outside expert), taking an instant photo (such as a Polaroid) for the purpose of determining the composition you want on a final photo, photographing employees for employee files, newsletters, or "employee of the month" award, or a variety of other purposes. You most likely will need a good 35 mm camera with macro, telephoto, and wide-angle lenses; a Polaroid camera for instant photos; a copy stand taking stills of products and printed materials; a tripod; and a variety of color and black and white indoor and outdoor films.

HEADLINE FILE.

You should keep all good headlines you find or create in a notebook. The ones you create can be reviewed and used at a later time, and the ones that you have found can be used to inspire creative ideas.

MEDIA BUYING GUIDES.

To select the proper media for an ad you plan to run, there are a variety of different guides published by various companies. Adweek's Marketer's Guide To Media is one such publication (49 E. 21st Street, NY, NY 10010, 212-995-7275). It describes all the various media in detail giving rates and audience information so that you can select the appropriate media to reach your target market. Of course you should always do some simple research on your own. The best is to get a consensus from customers and target prospects as to the publications they most frequently read.

PERSONNEL FILE.

You should maintain a file of consulting, graphics, copyrighting, photography, typography and other personnel whom you can contact quickly whenever you need them. Even if you are doing most of your own marketing, there will be times when you are inundated with work and you need to hire outside help on a temporary basis. Rather than bury these in a file cabinet, it's a good idea to keep them in a notebook in alphabetical order by subject matter and name. For example all photographers will be listed in alphabetical order behind the "PHOTOGRAPHERS" Tab in the notebook.

While there are many other tools used from time to time, the above list should serve as a good starting point. You may need only a few of the items listed above (especially if you have an automated system), or you may need additional tools that aren't listed for your particular purposes. Whatever your needs, your tool chest will become customized to your own personal needs as you undertake the specific requirements of each project. Having knowledge of the various automated systems, mechanical implements, measuring tools, papers, inks, guides, and files will enable you to better understand the process and to create better marketing pieces. The more you know, the more you will be able to use, and the greater the diversity and creativity of your marketing pieces.

With this basic introduction to the tools you will need and the foundation provided by the UMS, the Creation Cycle, and the Marketing process of previous Chapters, you should be ready to start applying these basics to the creation of specific types of marketing pieces for your organization. We will start with one of the most popular types of marketing pieces — the print ad.

SUGGESTED EXERCISES.

1. Locate typographers, printers, and graphics design houses in your local Yellow Pages.

2. You are going to go on a sort of "scavenger hunt" with the purpose of building your files of necessary tools. You are going to want to get the following: Type specifications book, Paper samples book, and Color Specifications Guide.

3. Make some phone calls to the companies you have located in step one. Tell them that you are responsible for marketing in your organization and that you need to collect the above-listed items in order to do your job. You might also mention that you are looking for good typographers, printers, and graphics design houses to use when the need arises.

4. While you have them on the phone, you may want to ask them if they give out forms rulers, Haberules, etc. for promotional purposes. Many companies do hand them out as promotions with their name, address and phone numbers on them.

5. Collect the necessary items plus any other goodies you find. Add them to your tool chest.

6. Enter those companies and people who were most helpful in your hunt in your Personnel File. This file can take the form of a rolodex, notebook, business card file, or some other form that is most comfortable for you. You might even one to keep this information in more than one place (i.e. in a rolodex for the office and in a notebook which you can take with you on business trips or when you work at home).

7. Keep your eyes open for other tools which you might need and for outside personnel that you might to add to your Personnel File. Add them as you find them.

Chapter 8 • PRINT MEDIA ADS

"Nobody said it is going to be easy..."

IT'S A REAL CHALLENGE.

When you think about it, creating an effective ad is a real challenge. Just to play the game, you must come up with a lot of money for a very small space in a publication which your research (if you've done any) tells you is the best vehicle to reach your target audience. In this small space, you must grab the target audience's attention, communicate the main point(s) of the ad, and solicit a buying action. This would be difficult even if there were no other obstacles in the way. However, there are obstacles. Many other companies have ads in the same publication, and everyone is competing for the choicest locations — *inside cover, back cover, before the center fold,* and/or *right-hand placement.* Furthermore, whatever location they give you (most publications won't guarantee a specific location), readers are going to subconsciously compare your ad with others in the same issue.

These obstacles are not being discussed here to scare you, but to make you aware of the magnitude of the challenge and to get your adrenaline flowing. Too many marketers look at the creation of ads as a routine job. Unfortunately, their ads often have the look of mediocrity— especially since they copy or recycle ad ideas from competitors and others. Such ads get lost in the crowd. Adrenaline can do wonders for creativity. Remembering that the competition is tough and the stakes are high should put you in the right frame of mind so you'll "take your best shot" and do the very best you can. With this introduction, let's look at the important considerations in creating a print ad.

KEEP THE FUNDAMENTALS IN MIND.

When creating an ad, or any marketing piece, you should always keep the fundamentals in mind. While this may seem obvious, many forget them when creating ads. They lose sight of the main objectives, and get lost in their own creativity. There are three sets of fundamentals that are most important. They are: (1) General marketing principles such as the seven building blocks of marketing — the 5Ps, Corporate Image, and the Marketing Information System, (2) The UMS, and (3) The Creation Cycle. After using the *Marketing Plan* as a *blueprint*, the first set gives you the basic foundation. The second provides the structure, and the third ties it all together and provides you with the timing, or the sequence of necessary steps.

UNDERSTAND THE CHARACTERISTICS OF A SUCCESSFUL AD.

While we have discussed the structure of a successful ad in the Chapter on the UMS, we can enhance our understanding of what makes a successful ad by looking at it from a slightly different angle — that is, from the perspective of the characteristics of a successful ad. The successful ad:

Hooks or draws the reader in. While we've "beat this concept to death", we can never repeat it enough times.

Has a strong visual appeal. An ad with strong visual appeal can hook the reader even if the headline is not particularly strong. The old wisdom — "a picture is worth a thousand words" — can be true if it's a good picture.

Is easy to read and understand. Good ads place the interests of the target audience first and foremost. Making it easy for your audience to read and understand your ad is the first step in convincing them that you are concerned with their welfare. Boring them to death or confusing them with a complicated message shows little or no concern. More importantly, if it is easy to read and understand, your message has a better chance of getting through to the widest number of market targets. In addition to getting through and communicating concern, it also communicates something about the competence of your company. Many readers feel that if you can't write an ad that is easy to read and understand, it is unlikely that you'll have the competence to make easy-to-use products that work as represented.

Is interesting. Again, thinking of the readers and the 20,000+ messages to which they are exposed each week, the most successful ads are interesting and even fun to read.

Focuses on the proper audience. Ads which focus on market targets are most successful. The reasons include the following: (1) Market targets take notice since they know you are speaking to them; (2) Prospective buyers assume that your products have been developed to meet their specific needs; and (3) Your marketing dollars are not wasted on prospects who are not interested in your products.

Talks one-on-one or person-to-person. Ads are more successful if they talk to market targets one-on-one. People buy from companies with which they are comfortable. You can make them more comfortable by writing the ad in a style which communicates with each prospect individually. Use of "You" rather than the less personal "They", "Them", "People", "Customers", etc. can serve this end.

Makes believable claims. Ads that lie or deceive, don't work. Truthful ads which are hard to believe don't either. Successful ads communicate product benefits in a logical and believable fashion. Unproven superlatives should never be used. If superlatives such as "We are number one..." or "We are the best, fastest, smallest, largest..." are used, they should be accompanied by proof. Proof can be provided in many ways. The most common include: providing product specifications and comparing them with those of the competition; quoting well-known, credible independent authorities (i.e. winner of the *Pulitzer prize, Academy award, Grammy award,* or judged "best buy" by *Consumer Reports Magazine*); and customer case histories or testimonials (they are perhaps the most effective since prospects believe their peers over company advertisers).

Follows a logical format. Successful ads have a *beginning, middle and end.* They usually read from *left to right* and from *top to bottom.* They are clean looking, and communicate the main messages of the ad in logical fashion. Ads which don't present selling messages in a logical fashion communicate disorganization, chaos, lack of professionalism, lack of know-how, and other "bad things" about the company and its products.

Focus on what you are selling. Successful ads have a clear selling objective. They emphasize important points in an effort to achieve the selling objective which is usually to sell the product or solicit a buying action which will lead to the sale of the product. They focus on the product being sold, and don't confuse the reader by introducing other products or objectives. Company logos and slogans which are too large, misplaced, or unrelated to the main message of the ad will only destroy the focus and confuse the reader. Confused prospects either postpone their buying decisions or fall prey to clearer messages presented by your competition.

Portrays a positive customer-oriented image. The most effective ads are positive, don't directly "bad-mouth" the competition, and portray the company as being customer oriented. They make every effort to establish a positive and long-lasting relationship with members of the target audience. Ads which are negative, boastful, company-centric and/or derogatory act as a mirror which negatively reflects on your company and products.

UNDERSTAND THE OBJECTIVES OF THE AD.

With these characteristics and fundamentals as a backdrop, it is important to establish and clearly understand the specific objectives of the ad. These objectives usually involve selling something. This "selling something" often takes on different forms including one or more of the following: to position, encourage prospects to take a buying action, inform, communicate, create an image, answer an objection, congratulate, announce a new product, or change a name or an image. As a basis for understanding these objectives, you should review the marketing plan and pay particular attention to the positioning and promotion strategies. After your review, you should confirm your understanding of the specific objectives of the piece with the top marketing decision makers in your organization. In addition to being politically smart, it is the right thing to do — especially since they are the ones who are ultimately responsible for the piece.

AD HEADLINE.

Once all of the above are clearly understood, you should create the headline in accordance with the objective(s) of the piece. As explained in previous chapters, the headline should contain the main message of the ad and/or hook the readers into reading and understanding the main message of the ad. It is very important for the ad headline to have an effective hook — even more important than in other types of marketing pieces. The reason is that, unlike a brochure, product description, or seminar invitation, the ad headline has to compete with many other ads in the same publication. It has to grab the reader's attention so that the reader is motivated to pause and read the ad before turning the page and reading an article or another ad.

Often times ad headlines work together with a photo or graphic to communicate the message of the ad. If possible, it's best to create the ad headline so that it can stand alone. The reason is that a stand alone headline is usually stronger and more effective. Furthermore, it can be used in other marketing pieces and become a trademark or an effective slogan which can be used on product packaging, promotional items, and as a company identifier. Avis's "We try harder" headline was so effective that it served such multiple purposes.

There are many techniques to help you think of a good line. If you're good at creating good headlines, you probably don't need much help. If you're a novice or feel you need improvement there are some steps you can follow that should help.

Find Effective Headlines. You should keep a file of "good" ads. Whenever you find an ad that has a particularly effective headline, tear it out of the newspaper or magazine (or make a copy if you have a copy machine handy), and put it in a file under the heading "GOOD ADS". Various magazines such as "Adweek's Marketing Week" (published by A/S/M Communications, Inc. 49 E. 21st Street, New York, NY 10010, 212-529-5100) sometimes rate ads and give reasons why the ads are good or bad. You should scan these issues and file the pages which refer to why ad headlines are effective or not. Before you know it, you'll be able to replicate the various techniques used by master headline writers.

Write down key words. You should write down the key words of the message you want to convey to your target markets. Don't copy your competitors. Remember you want to "stand out" from the field rather than blend in.

Manipulate those words into meaningful phrases. Play around with the words until you have catchy, concise and meaningful lines. Keep all the prospective headlines in a notebook which you can simply title "Headlines". Even if you don't use them for this piece, you may want to call on them in the future.

Refer to "Creating Effective Hooks." Refer to Chapter 5 on "Creating Effective Hooks" for suggestions.

Refer to Books on the Subject. There are interesting books on the subject of writing effective ad copy. One popular book is Words that Sell by Richard Bayan (published by Contemporary Books, Inc., Chicago and New York 1984).

Test your lines on others. Don't be guilty of pride of authorship. Many of us just "love" whatever we do. Remember it's not what we think that is important; it's what prospects, or market targets, think that is of paramount importance. Therefore, test your headlines on prospects in your target audience. While they may not know why, they'll tell you if you have a headline which is particularly effective. When you run the test, however, you should give them several choices and not tell them the ones that you like best.

HEADLINE EXAMPLE.

Keeping these techniques in mind, let's create a headline for an ad.

We will fill out the basic project information on a *Marketing Piece Set-Up Form*. This form is a handy tool to use on all marketing projects. After it's completed it should be kept in a notebook in job name sequence. Let's complete this form for our example in *Figure 8-1* below.

MARKETING PIECE SET-UP FORM

Job Number: CPL-121480

Job Name: Lawyer Testimonial Ad

Company/Division: COMPAL, INC. (Please note: The author of this book was the former Vice President of Marketing and the President of this Corporation and is using this information with permission from the Corporation. Certain information, such as the phone number, is *fictitious.*).

Address: P.O. BOX 67A11, Los Angeles, CA 90067

Phone: 213-7COMPAL. Contact person: Mary Ellen Ambrose

Company Business: Manufactures and markets turnkey microcomputer systems for business.

Product(s): *Compal 8200* and *EzType* computer and word processing systems, *Electric Briefcase* portable computer.

Market targets for this ad: Lawyers.

Objectives of piece: To initiate a buying action (to call, stop in, or write) on the part of the market targets. To capitalize on testimonials from customers.

Figure 8-1

After completing the form, we begin to create the headline.

Keywords. First we write down key words. Key words include: *Lawyers, Law Firms, Computers, Word Processors, Legal, Law, Attorneys, Testimonial,* and *Compal.*

Meaningful phrases. Next we manipulate these key words into the following meaningful phrases which communicate the kind of messages we wish to transmit to the target audience.
- *Here's what lawyers have to say about Compal systems.*
- *Lawyers give expert testimony on Compal Computer Systems.*
- *Attorneys testify on behalf of Compal Computer Systems.*
- *The legal word on Compal Computers.*
- *Why successful lawyers choose Compal.*

We think about the above phrases, ask the opinions of customers and prospects who are attorneys, and decide to select *"Lawyers Give Expert Testimony on Compal Computer Systems."* "It identifies the target market, the company and the product and uses a "play on words" hook since "testimony" is a legal term and serves to identify the ad as a testimonial ad.

Combined with an effective reinforcing photo, this headline can be extremely effective in grabbing attention and staying in the minds of attorneys who are in the market for a computer.

BODY TEXT.

After we compose the headline we work on the body text of the ad.

Lots of space. We know that good ads usually have plenty of space — so our main points stand out and don't get lost. Therefore, we want to use as few words as possible in the body text to convey the messages we want our target audience to read and remember. To insure that your body text is concise, it is a good practice to revise it several times. A good rule to remember is when in doubt, cut it out.

For the reader's convenience. We also want to design the ad for the convenience of the reader. This means that we should highlight the main points by boldfacing, italicizing, and/or indenting them. In this way, the busy reader can "pick up" the main points without having to read the entire ad.

Read like a story. Even though we will be highlighting the main points of the ad, we would like the ad to read like a coordinated story for those readers who choose to read the entire ad.

Tie-in with headline. We also want the body to flow directly from the headline and to tie in with the headline, the sub-headlines, and the photos or graphics used in the ad. In this

Emphasize benefits to the reader. The body of the ad explains and supports the main points. Rather than emphasize technical features which some readers may not understand, the body should focus on benefits which everyone understands.

With this understanding of the body text of an ad, lets continue with our example.

BODY TEXT EXAMPLE.

As stated in our ad objectives, we want to use some of the testimonials in our file. Testimonials are a very effective way of marketing your product since they show that there are happy customers who feel positive enough about the product to write nice things about it and to lend their endorsements in print. We select three short testimonials that are representative of attorneys with name recognition that are located in different geographical areas in our prime market territory.

After making the selection, we send legal releases to the three customers who will be featured in the ad to sign. In the "sue-crazy" era we live in, we don't want any trouble before, during or after the ad is published. A sample of a simple release form which is commonly used is shown below in *Figure 8-2*. You should check with your legal counsel before using this form since the author and publisher of this book are not responsible for its applicability to your particular situation or for changes in laws that may take place.

STANDARD RELEASE FORM.

This is to grant to (**YOUR COMPANY NAME** goes here) the right to use without restriction in (**YOUR COMPANY NAME** goes here)'s promotional materials my words, likeness and name.

Customer's Name: _____   **Phone:** _____

Company Name: _____   **Fax:** _____

Street Address: _____

City: _____   **ST:** ____   **Zip:** _____

Signature: _____   **Date:** _____

Figure 8-2

Once the releases are sent, we work on composing our body text that will accompany the testimonial quotes.

After several iterations and re-writes, we decide on the following for our body text.

Lawyers agree that Compal small computers save them time and money. In fact, most find that a Compal pays for itself within six months.

That's because a Compal system is powerful enough to handle a growing law office's word processing, billing, calendering and accounting. Faster and easier than you ever thought possible.

Just call your local Compal showroom today for a free demonstration. And personally witness what a Compal can do for you.

BODY TEXT ANALYSIS.

Notice that the body identifies the market targets and uses the marketing principles of positioning, product, and price. It uses these variables in harmony with each other. That is, the affordability of the product is communicated in such a way that it does not compromise the position or quality image of the product. The concept of price is described in terms of return on investment and payback rather than dollars. This avoids the need to scrap the ad if prices change (which they frequently do in the computer business) and guards against readers rejecting the product merely on the basis of advertised price (there's always someone who has a lower advertised price). The body text talks about the capabilities and benefits of the product without confusing readers with a lot of needless technical jargon. It communicates the benefits of speed, ease of use, and power by allowing the reader to define these benefits in his/her own terms ("...powerful enough to handle a growing law office's... Faster and easier than you ever thought possible."). It flows directly into the close.

CLOSE.

The close of the ad is extremely important. As you recall from the Chapter on the Universal Marketing Structure the close should do the following:

Tie in. All closes should tie-in with the headline. A masterful close will tie in with both the headline and the body text. The idea is that it is the *last main idea* left in the reader's mind. It should therefore reinforce the main message(s) of the ad.

End the ad. As its name implies, the close should end the story of the ad. It should not leave the reader "hanging in mid air" or in the middle of an unfinished thought. Many immature ads continue with significant amounts of text after the close. This is usually a mistake. It causes confusion and implies that your company is disorganized. The signature section of the ad, containing the logo and/or slogan plus "small print" disclaimer information is the only text that should follow the close.

Solicit Action. The close should solicit action — usually a buying action where you ask the reader to call, stop in, write, or send in a coupon for more information. The type of action is determined by the objectives of the piece as delineated in the *Marketing Piece Set-up Form* of *Figure 8-1*.

Provide a Marketing Information System mechanism. Most companies don't have a system to measure the effectiveness of their ads, but they should. If a coupon is included in the ad, it should be coded so that you can determine the exact issue of the publication in which the ad appeared. Even if there is no coupon, clever ads will ask readers to bring in a copy of the ad to their local dealer or quote a special code name or number when they call or write in.

CLOSE EXAMPLE.

Continuing with our example, we compose the following close for our ad.

> *"Just call your local Compal showroom today for a free demonstration. And personally witness what a Compal can do for you."*

CLOSE ANALYSIS.

The close flows directly from the body. Consistent with our stated objectives, it solicits a buying action by asking prospects to "call for a free demonstration." It uses the marketing variables of product *("...demonstration..."* and *"...what a Compal can do for you.")* price and promotion *("free demonstration").* While not listed above, beneath the close, we want to use the distribution marketing variable by listing the various places the prospect can call, write, or stop in to take a buying action. The close ties in with the legal theme of the text and headline of the ad by using a play on words to ask the audience to *"...witness what a Compal can do for you."*

SIGNATURE.

The signature helps to graphically frame the ad. It also gives the ad finality and identity by signing the ad with the company logo.

SIGNATURE EXAMPLE.

The Compal logo is always placed in the lower right corner of the ad (where signatures should be because they are the last main item on the page) at a 45-degree angle (to attract more attention). It consists of the name **"COMPAL"** in **Helvetica bold** type and all caps with ᴄᴏᴍᴘᴜᴛᴇʀ ꜱʏꜱᴛᴇᴍꜱ in light Helvetica type and all caps one-sixth the size of the COMPAL name.

PHOTO.

The photo should be graphically interesting, picture the product in the very best light possible, and should reinforce the headline and other main points of the ad.

In most cases, if people are going to be used in the ad, they should be professional models who know how to properly communicate ad themes in their expressions and body language.

If the product is good looking, you want to shoot it showing as much definition as possible. If the product is not good looking, you want to distort the photo with special lenses and/or use patterned screens to give the photo a distorted and/or artistic look.

PHOTO EXAMPLE.

In the case of the Compal ad, to make the photo graphically interesting, we decide to shoot it from above. We also decide to use a professionally-dressed woman so that readers can define her role as they see it (either as an attorney or a secretary), depending on the way they think. We shoot the photo in a photographer's studio with a white background and no horizon or walls (no angles) to graphically interfere with the body text. Because we are using a professional model and the product is reasonably good looking, we shoot the photo with a "normal" lens which gives an undistorted view of the scene.

In the photo session, we take many shots with a Polaroid camera to test the lighting and the composition. When we get the composition the way we want it and we find the angles we like, we take many different 35mm shots.

Once the shots are developed, we get several opinions from people in the target audience, add our own two cents, and choose the shot we are going to use.

SELECT MEDIA.

Before we can finalize the layout and choose the type, we must select the most important publications in which this ad will run. The reason is that different publications have different space, or mechanical, requirements. Once we have the mechanical specifications of our number one choice, we can finalize the layout and size and fit the type and the photo for our selection. If we decide to run this same ad in several different publications, we may have to make some changes if the mechanicals are markedly different. If they are similar (i.e. if the have the same proportions) we can easily enlarge or reduce the ad slick. Otherwise, we may have to re-do the layout for certain publications.

Too often, companies don't spend enough time and effort researching the best media for meeting the objectives of the ad. All print media *keep information on their readership.* You should research this information before making a selection. The idea is to *match the characteristics of your target audience as closely as possible with the media's readership.* Selection criteria typically include the following:

Audience size. You'd like to know the circulation, or number of people the publication reaches. All organizations need the proper coverage to generate enough leads to make their sales numbers.

Demographics. You'd like to know the breakdown of this audience according to age, sex, income levels, disposable income, buying preferences, and other specific characteristics.

Geographic Coverage. You'd like to know if the territory which the publication covers matches the locations of your target markets. If you are selling product in only one state, you need not waste money by advertising in a national publication. Conversely, if your audience is national or international, you don't want to buy just local coverage.

Image of the Publication. It is important that the image of the publication fits with the positioning of your product. You want to make sure that your product does not take on any adverse effects by virtue of its association with publications that have images of inferior quality or strong political affiliations.

Print Quality. With regard to magazines, the quality of print can affect the quality of your ad. You should therefore try to insure that the positioning of your product in synch" with the print quality of the publication.

Mechanical Requirements. You need to know the mechanical requirements of the publication in order to finalize the ad. *"Mechanicals"* refer to such criteria as page size, column size, lines per page, characters to the inch, type of screens used on photos, etc. Sometimes the mechanical requirements can affect the overall look of quality of the ad.

Cost. As with all business decisions, the cost of ad space is very important. It has to fit within the marketing budget, and it serves as one of the valuable inputs for determining the effectiveness (return on investment) of the ad. Cost of ad space is typically measured in *CPM*, or cost per thousand prospects reached. Ad space that costs a little more might reach many more market targets — yielding a much lower cost per thousand, or CPM. Costs of ad space is provided in media directories published by various companies and in rate cards provided directly from the publication. For those publications which you plan to use frequently, it is a good idea to keep rate cards on file since they often contain the mechanical requirements of the publication in addition to rates for ad space.

After making your media selection, the next task is to select an appropriate location within the chosen publication. Many publications keep statistics on the effectiveness of various locations. You should investigate these statistics if they are available. Without knowing the specific publication, you should already know that the best locations are typically, the inside front cover, the back cover, the center fold, before the center fold, and right-hand placement (i.e. pages on the right). If the publication is doing an editorial on your product or company, a good location might be on or near one of the related editorial pages.

MEDIA SELECTION EXAMPLE.

Returning to our ad example, we want a publication that is faithfully read by prospects in our market territory. Compal primarily covers Southern California, but also has significant attorney customers in Northern California. Upon considering the criteria above and reviewing the various alternatives, we make the decision that the best publication for reaching our target market is the Parker Directory of California Attorneys. It is used by most legal personnel in California because it lists all the courts, judges, attorneys, etc. for each county in California. It has a long "shelf" life since it is revised only once per year. According to our market research, it has the most accurate mailing list of attorneys in California. In addition, there are not too many ads in the publication to dilute the effect of the Compal ad. What's more, the cost per thousand prospects reached is the lowest of all the other possible choices.

FINALIZE LAYOUT AND TYPE.

As shown in the *Parker Directory rate and mechanical card* shown in *Figure 8-3*, a full-page ad measures 6" wide by 8".

RATE CARD & MECHANICAL GUIDELINES

DISPLAY RATES

VOLUMES I & II
*PREFERRED POSITIONS

❖ **Front Inside Cover** (1/2 Page) $2910.00
❖ **Back Inside Cover** (1/2 Page) $1560.00
❖ **Divider Card** (Full Page) $1980.00
❖ **Top of Page Listings** $20.00 per page

*These positions are subject to renewal by existing advertisers.

VOLUME II

❖ **1/4 Page** (6" wide X 2") $575.00
❖ **1/2 Page** (6" wide X 4") $905.00
❖ **Full Page** (6" wide X 8") $1650.00

EXPERT WITNESS SECTION

❖ **1/4 Page** (5 1/4" wide X 1 3/4") $250.00
❖ **1/2 Page** (5 1/4" wide X 3 1/2") $475.00
❖ **Full Page** (5 1/4" wide X 7 1/8") $875.00

Requirements
All ads must be camera-ready (stat or pasteup) and submitted before August 31, 1988.
Confirmation and Remittance forms will be sent upon receipt of the Return Mail Card.
Publication Trim size is 7" X 9". Halftones are 133 line screens. Ads are printed by
offset. Negatives submitted will be charged cost of making camera-ready.

Figure 8-3

Based on these dimensions we determine that, in order to fit our layout, our headline copy will be 24-point (2 picas or 1/3 of an inch), and our body text will have to be 6-point.

To give proper emphasis to our text and to coordinate with the Compal logo, we decide to put our testimonial quotes in **Helvetica boldface italic** type. We put them in one column on the left. In the right column, we put the main body text in "normal" (up and down) Helvetica type. Since we only have a small amount of text we decide to emphasize main points in the body text by paragraph indentations rather than boldfaced subheads. In this case, with the short amount of text, boldfaced subheads would look bad graphically and would interfere with the bold-faced testimonial quotes on the left. Moreover, boldfaced quotes would take up too much unnecessary space and make the ad look too crowded.

In our original dummy, we put the photo between the headline and body text. However, after playing around with the layout, we decide to put the body text immediately after the headline. This new placement improves the flow and the look of the ad. The camera angle of the photo and the shape of the computer desk make the photo look much better below.

We decide to visually tie the headline, testimonials, body text and photo together with a light gray screen. As shown in the mechanical requirements provided in *Figure 8-3*, the *Parker Directory* uses a 133-line screen for halftones. For contrast (and because the *Compal logo* background is normally reversed to highlight the 45-degree angle), we decide to put the *Compal logo* and the distribution locations outside the light gray screen. In this way, they do not visually interfere with the main points of the ad, but they are there in the proper location to work for us in the ad.

PRODUCE THE MECHANICAL AND THE AD SLICK.

Once we finalize the layout and get all the pieces of our ad, we create our camera-ready mechanical to meet the specific requirements for the Parker Directory. We go through bluelines, final approvals and all the steps of the Creation Cycle to compose the final ad slick. Once completed, we send the ad slick, or the mechanical camera-ready art, to the Parker Directory with instructions to return it when they are finished with it. A copy of the finished ad is shown in *Figure 8-4*.

AUDIT.

After they run the ad, they send us tear sheets which are actual copies of the ad that is run in the directory. We also request at least one whole copy of the completed directory for our records and our reference. We don't pay for the ad unless we are satisfied that no mistakes were made in the presentation or the quality of the ad.

EFFECTIVENESS MEASUREMENT.

Since there is only one issue of this Directory each year, there was no need to code the ad for measuring its effectiveness. We simply train all personnel who answer the phone or greet walk-ins to ask the prospect how they heard of Compal and to write the answer on a *Lead Card* — see *Figure 8-5*. At the end of each month, all the leads, appointments and sales generated by this ad will be tallied along with those generated by other promotional sources on a Promotion Effectiveness Report — see *Figure 8-6*. The cost effectiveness of all promotional sources will be tracked. The effective ones (those that generate sales) will continue to receive the company's marketing dollars. Those that are ineffective will be studied in greater detail (their ineffectiveness may be the result of seasonality, a poor ad, or other factors that are not the fault of the publication). They will be dropped if it is determined that they are not a good source for generating sales. In this way, the company will know not continue to throw good money away on ineffective media.

TESTIMONIAL AD

Figure 8-4

LEAD CARD

Front

ENCORE VIDEO INDUSTRIES

Name: _____ Date: _____

Position: _____

Firm: _____

Address: _____

_____ Zip: _____

Business phone _____ Other phone _____

Comments:

Where did you hear about us?   **System Type**

☐ newsletter _____   ☐ word of mouth _____   ☐ EPR
☐ show _____   ☐ seminar/speech _____   ☐ PRISM
☐ sales call _____   ☐ mailing _____   ☐ FVS 100
☐ magazine _____   ☐ other _____   ☐ other _____

Back

Follow Up History

Figure 8-5

PROMOTION EFFECTIVENESS REPORT

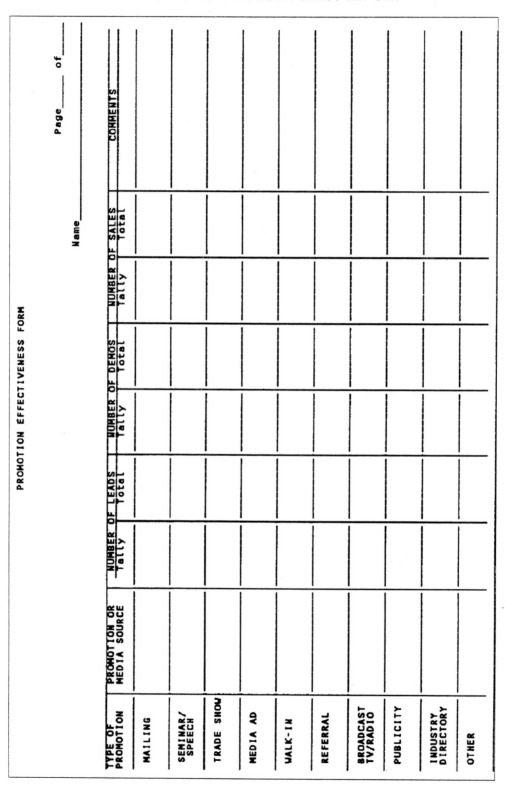

Figure 8-6

PRINT AD SUMMARY.

Print ads can be a very effective means of achieving the organization's marketing objectives. As you can see, there are so many factors to be considered that a rational analytical approach has to be applied if you are to be successful in the long run. Creating print ads by the "seat of your pants" will not produce consistent results. You have to follow the foundation and structures provided by marketing principles, the UMS, and the other concepts discussed in prior Chapters. As a summary, the important points to remember when creating print ads include the following:

1. Objectives for the ad should be determined in accordance with the Marketing Plan, and they should be approved by decision makers.

2. The look of the ad has to be in harmony with positioning of the product in the ad. For example to communicate a quality position, the ad and the product in the ad should have a quality look. To market a high-tech product, the graphics and colors in the ad should be high-tech.

3. The print ad has to work harder than other types of marketing pieces because it has to compete for attention with many other ads in the same publication.

4. Headlines and hooks have to be particularly effective. Unlike brochures and other marketing pieces that have a lot of competition in the same publication.

5. Body text has to flow from the headline, communicate product benefits, tie-in with the headline and picture, and flow into the close.

6. Photos should tie-in with the headline and body of the ad, enhance rather than detract from the ad, communicate the product in the best light possible, and be visually appealing and interesting.

7. If the products are not particularly good looking, they can be made more interesting and appealing with special lenses and patterned screens.

8. If people are used in the ad, they should be professional models or at least people with experience being photographed by a camera.

9. Ads should be designed and/or coded so their effectiveness can be more easily measured.

10. In general, ads should grab attention, stay in the reader's mind, and cause a buying action.

As you create more and more ads, you will be surprised at how easy the process becomes. For now, you may a little overwhelmed. If you are, this merely means that you need more practice and experience. The best way to get experience is by "rolling up your sleeves" and creating ads — lot's of ads. For practice, the end-of-chapter exercises below should help you.

The better you learn to create effective ads, the better you'll do in creating other marketing pieces. The reason is simple. Most of the principles and concepts are the same. They use the same foundations and structures. To reinforce your learning of them, many principles and concepts will be repeated throughout the text as they are applicable. To avoid too much redundancy, however, the remainder of the chapters will concentrate on those principles, concepts and techniques which are unique to the particular marketing piece being discussed.

The next Chapter focuses on creation of the product brochure.

SUGGESTED EXERCISES.

1. Pull a "good" ad out of the "Good Ads" file that you should be keeping.

2. Create an ad (a dummy or rough is sufficient) for your company/product which uses the principles and concepts incorporated in these ads.

3. As you are creating your ad, continue to ask yourself what makes the professional ads so effective. Try and relate these effective elements to the *UMS* and the *seven building blocks*.

4. Create two dummies from two of the other good ads in your file. Without telling them which is yours, show your dummy along with the two dummies made from the professional ads to one or two people in your target audience (you can substitute friends if you need to).

5. Ask them which one they like the best and to identify the reasons why. Make sure you understand their reasons and incorporate them the next time you create your next ad. If they don't like yours, make sure you don't take the criticism personally. Even the best ad writers are criticized for some of their work. Moreover, you're just learning. Conversely, make sure that you "don't let it go to your head" if they like yours the best.

Chapter 9 • BROCHURES

"Everyone's got at least one..."

While some organizations never do a print ad, almost all develop a brochure for one purpose or another.

WHAT IS IT?

A brochure is a booklet-style marketing piece, usually from one to eight pages in length, which describes your product, product line, and/or company in some detail. It is usually given or mailed to prospects in response to their expressed interest in your company and its products. This interest may have been generated by a print ad, referral, Yellow Pages Ad, walk-in or some other contact with your company.

Sometimes brochures are sent to target prospects unsolicited in an effort to generate new leads. However, the brochures used for this purpose should be lighter weight, more concise and less expensive versions of your main company and product brochures. They are often designed to be self-mailers or to fit in standard business-sized envelopes. Their objective is to generate initial interest in your company and products (i.e. generate leads) rather than respond to an already expressed interest. Because of their different character, they will be discussed in a subsequent Chapter on Mailers. This Chapter will concentrate on your main company and product brochures which are designed for "qualified leads" (those prospects who have already expressed an interest in your products and your company).

Since these brochures usually serve as the centerpiece of the marketing effort for your company's products, they are more expensive and more substantial than the self-mailer variety. They are typically printed on more expensive, heavier-weight brochure stock in an 8.5 by 11-inch format. As such, they are designed to be handed to the prospect by a sales person or mailed in a large envelope along with a personally written cover letter.

Because of their importance, such brochures often contain background information on your company (history, business philosophy, past successes, and service orientation) in addition to information on your products. This company background information is provided so that target prospects will feel comfortable with your company and products. Getting the prospect to feel comfortable is a prerequisite for building a relationship with the prospect, converting the prospect into a customer, and developing customer loyalty. This loyalty, in turn, generates repeat sales and "free" word-of-mouth referrals.

CHARACTERISTICS.

Unlike a print ad, a brochure has a personality and set of characteristics all its own. These characteristics are summarized below:

Size and length. Brochures are typically larger and have a greater number of pages than print ads, product description sheets, or most other marketing pieces. Because of the larger amount of space available, more information on the company and its products can be provided.

Sometimes, this larger space availability is a more of a curse than a benefit. Many unsophisticated marketers feel compelled to say too much and to fill up every square inch of available space with text. The ability to say more is good, the compulsion to say too much is not. The text of brochures should be concise and should employ lots of space just as the text of print ads. If too much text is cramped into too small of a space, the important points will be lost and readers will find the brochure to be too tedious to read. Cramped text also serves to communicate many negatives about the company including: everything the company has to say is in this one brochure, the company is too cheap, the company is too unsophisticated, the company has no concern for the customer because it shows little or no consideration for the reader of the brochure, etc.

Segmentation. Since brochures typically do have more text than ads, however, the text should be broken up into easy-to-read segments. This can be accomplished by creating meaningful sub-headlines which (1) serve as "hooks" that entice the reader to continue reading and/or (2) contain the most important points of the brochure. By capsulizing the most important points of the brochure in sub-headlines, you are showing concern for the busy (or lazy) reader who does not want to be forced to read the entire brochure to understand its main messages.

Objectives. As with print ads, brochures need to focus on clear objectives. Many marketers don't seem to understand this. With the greater amount of space available, they often lose sight of the main objectives of the brochure. As a result, too many brochures ramble and fail to achieve their objectives. The brochure should work hard to sell the product. The greater amount of space should be economically used to provide more details about the product. These details should support the main points and the main focus of the brochure.

Quality. Unlike the print ad, where the print quality is controlled by the publication, the quality of the brochure is completely under your control. The paper, the ink, the photographs, the art, the graphics, the colors, the folds, etc. all should exude the quality you want to reflect on your product and your company. If, for some reason, you decide that you do not want the brochure to have a quality look, you should make the reasons for your decision clear to prospects who receive the brochure. Effective brochures have been developed on inexpensive stock using inexpensive materials in cases where marketers have acknowledged, in the text of the brochure, that the budget for the brochure has been deliberately kept to a minimum in an effort to hold down costs and to pass savings on to customers.

Design. Whereas the size and shape of print ads are somewhat restricted by the mechanical requirements of the particular publication in which it appears, the design of the brochure has few restrictions. Some of the more important aspects of the design include the following:

Shape. While the outside shapes of most brochures are 8.5 by 11-inch rectangles oriented in the portrait direction (read from left to right along the smaller 8.5" dimension), brochures can come in virtually any shape imaginable. They often take the shape of the product which they represent. For example, there have been brochures used by companies in the recording industry that are in the shape of phonograph records. The author of this book developed a brochure for a portable computer named "The Electric Briefcase" in the shape of a briefcase with a handle. Auto brochures have come in the shape of the autos they sell. If you think about it, you probably can remember other examples of product-shaped brochures which you've seen.

While these brochures can be particularly effective in helping to sell the products which they represent, you should be aware of the price you may have to pay for this benefit. They cost a lot more to produce because they normally require (1) the development of a custom die to cut the brochure to the product shape; (2) a separate cutting process after the brochure is printed; and (3) special envelopes which have to be custom made. They often require special storage and handling because they are harder to stack and stuff into envelopes. They are more difficult to copy on a copy machine, and the resultant copies lose their unique shape. And, they are more difficult for your prospects to store in a file. Despite these disadvantages, however, if properly designed, these specially-shaped brochures can help to distinguish your products from the competition and can be more easily remembered by your prospects.

Size. While the most common size is 8.5" by 11", product brochures can come in virtually any size. The main advantage of a non-standard size is uniqueness. This uniqueness, in turn, helps the brochure's message to get in and stay in the prospect's mind. In the case of smaller brochures, an additional advantage is lower mailing costs. The primary disadvantages are the same as those described in the Shape Section above.

Color. Unlike print ads, you have complete control over the paper stock, the ink, and the printing of brochures. Because of this and the fact that brochures are typically printed on better quality stock than print ads, you have the ability to achieve exceptional color quality. To achieve exceptional color quality, however, you have to spend money on better printers and better materials.

Since 4-color is much more expensive than 2-color or black and white printing, you can save significant money by not printing in full color. Fortunately for those of us who like to save money, some of the best-looking and most artistic product brochures have been printed in black and white (note: the term "black and white" includes various shades of gray). Black and white brochures are particularly popular for high-tech products. A very effective use of color is to print most of the brochure in black and white and to add a single color for accents. Often, the single color matches the color of the product or product logo. When a single color is applied to the actual product in an otherwise black and white picture, it serves to make the product "stand out" even more. In addition to its use in brochures and print ads, this single-color technique has become very popular for TV commercials and poster displays.

Folds. Brochures can be folded in a variety of different ways depending on the number of pages in the brochure and the style you prefer. There are French folds, four-side folds, six-side folds, eight-side folds, accordion folds..., you name it. The most popular product brochures come with either 4 sides (11 by 17-inch stock folded down the middle to form four 8.5 by 11-inch sides) or six sides (11 by 25.5-inch stock folded twice at one-third points to form six 8.5 by 11-inch sides).

Believe it or not, the number and type of folds are not the only folding issues. The folding technique is also very important — particularly when using heavy stock that can fold unevenly or break apart at the fold. In such cases, the folds are "scored" in such a way that the paper stock folds properly.

Flaps and Pockets. Most print ads have to conform to the two-dimensional requirements of the publication page. Brochures have no such limitations. They can be designed with one or more flaps or pockets for inserting additional product litera-ture. If you are selling products whose design and specifica-tions change frequently, it is a good idea to use this flap design. The main brochure which holds the inserts can provide general company and product line information that is unlikely to change. Each insert can contain the product information that is likely to change, such as price lists and product specifications. In this way, there is no need to re-do the more expensive brochure folder when changes need to be made to one of the insert pages.

In addition to holding variable product information, flaps are handy for enclosing resumes of company personnel who will work on client projects, customer references, case histories, comparative information on the competition, price lists, and a variety of other information including cover letters. Often, two or four slits are cut in the flap or pocket so that a sales person's business card can be inserted. By using this flap/pocket design, a general brochure can have a long shelf life and change to the individual needs of the prospect. These are some of the advantages.

Disadvantages include the following: Because of its variability, some misuse the flap-style brochure by mixing incompatible items or enclosing too many sheets in one package; Flaps and pockets are much more expensive to produce; They are heavier and more expensive to mail — especially if they require over-sized envelopes; and Too many sales people have the compulsion to enclose too much information in one brochure — causing the recipient to be overwhelmed. As with all marketing decisions, however, these potential disadvantages have to be weighed against the benefits discussed above. The correct answer will be different depending on the specific needs of the company and the situation. Remember the decision criteria should be based on optimizing the return on your investment (i.e. the revenues generated versus the costs).

Paper Stock. As discussed before, the choice of paper stock is very important to the image projected. A quality message discussed in the brochure will be believed if the paper has the look of quality. This message will be questioned if the paper quality does not support what is said in the brochure. There are many decisions to be made in selecting paper stock. Some of the more relevant factors include: quality, weight, color, texture, sheen (if it's too shiny it may show all fingerprints) compatibility with the colors that will be printed, the ability to write notes on the surface, and the ability to fold without seriously fraying.

Depending on your specific purposes, your selections will vary.

Whatever your selections, it is strongly recommended that, if you are going to err, it should be on the side of better quality. Better quality paper holds the ink better, looks better, conveys a better image of your products and company, feels better to the touch, and lasts longer. When it comes to brochure stock, heavier is usually considered better. A relatively smooth surface is considered better quality. In most cases, lighter is preferred to darker.

If the cost trade-off is between doing the brochure in color or choosing quality paper stock, it is recommended that you do the brochure in black and white on good quality stock. If you need to cut costs further, reduce the number of pages in the brochure or cut out fancy shapes and sizes in favor of using better quality ingredients.

Photos and Art. In print ads, the use of photos and art are limited by the small amount of space available. Brochures are not so limited.

Photos should be used if they help to reinforce the main points of the brochure. As said before, a "picture can be worth a thousand words". However, you want the "thousand words" to enhance rather than detract from the main points in the brochure. That is, the pictures should be used if they serve a purpose. They shouldn't be used just for the purpose of including pictures in the brochure.

Pictures can serve a variety of useful purposes such as: showing the product in a favorable light; illustrating unique product features; showing the product being used in an actual work setting by market targets; reinforcing the main points or hooks contained in headlines; breaking up the text into easy-to-read sections; contributing to the graphics of the brochure; and making the product seem more real and tangible (this is particularly critical if you are marketing an intangible product or service).

If the products or subjects of the photo are not visually appealing, they should be artistically embellished with patterned screens or special-angle lenses or replaced by illustrations. A good photographer or graphic artist can make an unattractive product (whose unaltered photo would detract from the piece) very appealing.

Weight. The higher the weight of your brochure the more it will cost to mail. You should consider this when designing the brochure. As you might recall from the discussion on quality above, the heavier the brochure stock, the higher the perceived quality. This means that weight and quality are competing variables in brochure design. The ideal is to select the paper stock so that it just reaches the point of qualifying for good-quality status, but does not go "overboard" on the weight. It's not a bad idea to ask your paper vendor for various sample weights and to make "dummy" brochures which you will compare weights and determine the differences in resultant mailing costs. Over thousands of brochures the difference can be significant.

Handling Characteristics. The weight, the size, the color and many of the other design characteristics discussed above should be selected in accordance with the expected handling of the brochure. Many like the look of a glossy black brochure. Once they have them made, however, they are shocked to discover that such brochures look terrible once they are handled once or twice. They learn that every finger print and smear shows up on glossy dark backgrounds. This is only one of the problems that you should anticipate. You should also ask yourself the following questions about the eventual handling of the brochure:

- What if prospects want to take notes on the brochure? Will they be able to write on the surface? With ink? With pencil? Do you want them to be able to write on the surface?

- How will the edges and corners of the brochure look after it has been handled once or twice?

- What is the intended shelf life of the brochure? If it is expected to be long. The paper stock should be heavier rather than lighter.

- Do you expect brochures to be filed in a filing cabinet or stored in a 3-ring notebook? A 3-ring notebook may dictate wider margins so important information doesn't get lost where the punch holes will go.

- Do you want the brochure passed to different people in the target company or are you intending it to be kept by the person to which it is sent? You might want different decision makers in the same company to get their own brochure, or you might decide that one brochure should be passed around.

The point of the above is to make you aware of the importance of considering the handling of your brochure before finalizing the design. A perfectly good looking and effective brochure can be turned into an unattractive and ineffective remnant of its former self if these factors are not considered. If this happens, it could hurt rather than help your marketing and sales efforts.

One way to make some of the above decisions is to do some research as to how your brochures are likely to be handled. A few well-placed phone calls to existing customers and target prospects are likely to provide the proper answers. A review of how people in your company handle your vendor's brochures can also help. Another important step is to get paper stock samples and judge how they look after they are handled under actual conditions (holding, writing, filing, erasing, being exposed to rain and liquids, etc.).

Number of Pages. The more pages in the brochure, the greater the weight, the higher the typesetting, printing, folding, mailing, envelope, and filing costs. Furthermore, the more concise and clear the messages in the brochure, the more likely they will penetrate the minds of readers. These considerations beg for a fewer number of pages.

On the other hand, a significant number of readers like to have sufficient information in the brochure to adequately describe the product. It's also good to have adequate space, photos and graphics, and large enough letters for most readers to be able to easily read the text. These requirements tend to lengthen the number of pages.

While the number of pages in your brochure should accommodate the needs of your specific audience, it is strongly recommended that your brochure cover only the most important points and be as short as possible. If technical readers need more information, you can always send them specifications sheets, product manuals, and other more detailed information. You should remember that the brochure is a selling piece. As such, it should not ramble. The important points should not be lost in a sea of technical jargon or eloquent prose. Repeating a handy phrase used many times before, when in doubt, cut it out.

Effective brochures are often four to six pages. The four-page brochure typically has a cover page, two inside text and picture pages, and a back cover with over-flow text, product specifications, the company logo, address, and telephone number. It may also contain a return coupon for the prospect to send in for more information or to signal a sales person to call. The six-page brochure typically has the same format with two additional text and picture pages. If the brochure has more than eight sides, it will most likely have to be printed in signature and stapled at the fold (much the way a catalogue or magazine is bound together). The term signature refers to the process in which pages are printed in pairs. For example, the front and back cover are printed on the same piece of paper which is folded down the middle as are the first and last page, the second and next to last page, etc.

Having considered the above characteristics, it is now useful to go over what elements brochures should include.

WHAT THEY SHOULD INCLUDE.

A brochure is similar in format to an ad except that it usually contains more pages. As described above, it normally has a front and back cover with two or more pages inside. Most brochures include the following on each of each pages:

Cover

Headline. Like the print ad and other marketing pieces which follow the Universal Marketing Structure, the cover of the brochure should have a clear and concise headline with a strong hook. In those rare cases where a headline with a strong hook is considered inappropriate, the product name can be used. For example, "Introducing the new (product name goes here) from (company name goes here)".

Photo or Graphic. Following the headline, the brochure typically presents an interesting photo, illustration, or graphic which is representative of the company or product.

Sub-headline or Slogan. After the photo, the brochure may have a sub-headline, slogan, or follow-up phrase which ties in with the headline.

Logo. If not already included in the headline, the logo of the company and/or other company identifier should appear on the front cover. Although many novice marketers make the mistake of making the company identifier the most prominent element on the cover, the product and/or main message should be most prominent. Logos and company names that are too large make the company look amateurish and insecure. In a product brochure, they should be subordinate to the product and main message.

Inside

Features and Benefits. Inside the cover, the body text follows with the features and benefits of the product and the company. This body text is sectioned into easy-to-read text segments with highlighted sub-headlines (boldfaced, italicized, indented, inverse printed, or enlarged).

Credibility Information. In addition to features and benefits of the product, if applicable, the text should include information on your company's background and capabilities. Years in business, significant accomplishments, awards, philosophy of the founders, and background of key personnel (without identifying specific names) are the types of information typically provided.

Photos, illustrations, and graphics. Photos, illustrations and graphics are also used inside the cover to help section the text and reinforce the main messages of the brochure.

Close. As with print ads and other marketing pieces which follow the UMS, the brochure has a close which ties in with the main points and which solicits the reader to take a buying action. In those brochures where the back cover is reserved for product specifications, the close is typically positioned on the last page inside the cover.

Flap or Pocket. If the brochure has a flap or pocket for holding inserts, the flap typically appears on one or more of the inside pages. This flap may or may not have text copy and slits for inserting a business card.

Back Cover

Specifications. The back cover of most technical product brochures lists the product specifications. If the product does not lend itself to product specifications, the back cover may be blank or may merely be a continuation of the inside pages.

Logo. The company and/or product logos are typically located at the bottom of the back cover.

Distribution. Various company locations, addresses, and phone numbers are listed on the back cover. For those companies that are too large to list all offices worldwide, the main headquarters and/or some regional headquarters can be listed. It is important to have at least one address and phone number listed so that prospects can call, write or visit.

Return Coupon. Those brochures that have a return coupon usually put this coupon on the back cover or fold it over so that it is just inside the back cover. In the latter case, the coupon is usually a pre-paid self-mailer which can be easily torn off, filled out and mailed.

WHAT THEY SHOULDN'T INCLUDE.

Since most main company and product brochures can be very expensive to produce, they should not include information that is likely to change quickly. Such information often includes:

Prices. Prices are subject to change frequently. Even if they are not, it is not good form to include prices on a main brochure. Prices are typically quoted verbally, listed in a cover letter, or presented on separate price sheets.

Numbers that are likely to change. If the company knows it is going to move, those addresses and phone numbers that will soon be invalid should not be listed in the brochure unless, of course, there is no other choice.

Employees who may leave the company. With the high turnover rates in many companies, it is not a good idea to include photos of employees or even top executives. The reason is that the brochure could be rendered useless if they leave — especially if they go to a competitor.

Superlatives. This text has repeatedly warned of using unproven superlatives that claim your company is number one, the best, the fastest, etc. In a brochure, it is recommended that you also avoid proven superlatives. The reason is that competitors could easily render the brochure worthless and cause prospects to think you are lying to them by boosting their features — thereby making your superlative untrue. For example, even if your product is the fastest at the time you conceive of the brochure, by the time you print and distribute copies, competitors could have made speed improvements in their products which make your "fastest" claim untrue. This happens all the time.

Negatives. Since the brochure is the center piece of the company's marketing, it should not be negative, and it should not "bad-mouth" the competition. While negatives should be avoided in all marketing, they are particularly taboo in brochures because of their greater sense of permanence and closer association with the fabric of the company.

Competition. Many companies compare themselves with specific competitors in their brochures. This should be avoided in most cases. Firstly, it gives free advertising to the competitors. Secondly, it is usually considered amateurish — particularly if the competitors are industry leaders (for example, many companies compare themselves with IBM, and IBM doesn't need more recognition). Thirdly, competitors may change their names, be acquired by other companies, or go out of business — causing the reference to be confusing or totally useless.

With this understanding of what should and should not be in a brochure, it is useful to emphasize certain issues which are important to consider when designing your brochure.

FRONT COVER ISSUES.

As with most publications, the front cover is what "sells" the brochure.

You can judge a brochure by its cover

Since most brochures contain several pages, the entire cover serves the purpose of inviting the reader to turn the page. This is not to say that the headline is not important. It's to emphasize that the other elements of the cover are also important in attracting the reader to turn the page. Unlike the one page print ad, which has to grab readers who "thumb through" publications, brochure readers don't have the same immediate competition. The challenge is to get them to turn the page and to read what's inside, or at least read the main points inside. The competition comes later when they have the brochures of competitors and they compare them side by side.

Cover Alternatives

Printed. Most front cover elements are printed with ink on paper. This method offers perhaps the most versatility.

Photographed. Some front cover elements are photographic reproductions. This is particularly useful when a special photo-like glossy surface is desired.

Cut Out. Some cover elements are formed by "cut outs" in the front cover which reveal pictures or images on the next page. This gives a unique, three-dimensional effect to the brochure.

Embossed Surfaces. Another way to yield a 3-D effect is to emboss elements on the cover. This is typically done by making a die in the 3-D shape of the desired element(s). The cover is then pressed against the die to stamp out a raised-surface image on the front cover. If the 3-D image is left alone, the process is called blind embossing. Otherwise, ink or metallic foil is "printed" on the embossed surface. The company logo is an element that is often embossed on the front cover.

Stamped Surfaces. The inverse of embossing is stamping whereby the headline, picture, and or logo is stamped into the surface of the cover. The effect is similar to the stamping of names and images on the front cover and spine of a book binding.

The purpose of using one or more of these alternative methods is to create uniqueness and improve the company's image. Blind embossing and stamping give a classy look to the brochure. Cut outs give a high-tech look. Since these processes are typically more expensive than printing, they act as image enhancers which give the brochure a look of distinction.

BACK COVER.

While back covers don't get the attention of front covers, they still deserve your close attention. One reason is that brochures are often left on desks with their back covers up. Another is that they are often the last part of the brochure that will be seen and read.

As mentioned previously, they often contain such elements as: a continuation of the body text from the inside, product specifications, company distribution locations (addresses and phone numbers), logos, slogans, disclaimers, and copyright and trademark notifications. While many of these elements are not as exciting as front cover or inside elements, they are very important and should not be neglected.

Graphically, the back cover should be attractive and should complement the front cover.

The logo (with or without a company slogan) should be at the bottom to conclude, act as a company signature, and help to graphically frame the brochure. It should also serve to stamp a lasting image of the company and its products in the minds of the reader.

Other than product specifications, company locations and other supporting information, the back page should not introduce new ideas and concepts. It should be for summarizing and supporting what has already been said and for concluding the brochure.

With this understanding of the brochure, it is perhaps useful to look at an actual example.

BROCHURE EXAMPLE.

The brochure shown in *Figures 9-1 through 9-4* was created for Encore Video Industries, Inc., a high-tech start-up company. This company was founded to capitalize on the technology it developed to give its parent company, Encore Video, Inc., a proprietary advantage over its competitors in the post-production of commercials and episodic television shows. The product described in this brochure is named *EPR,* an acronym for *Electronic Pin Registration* (both EPR and Electronic Pin Registration are trademarks of Encore Video Industries, Inc.). EPR insures accuracy in the transfer of film to video tape. This accuracy, also called registration, is required for making quality video composites from multiple film elements. Competitive mechanical devices can also insure accuracy. However, they have two major disadvantages — (1) they are often prohibitively slow, and speed is essential in a business in which deadlines are critical and time is billed for several hundreds of dollars per hour, and (2) they engage the sprocket holes of the film with mechanical pins which can wear or endanger the film master (film masters are precious commodities often valued in the hundreds of thousands or millions of dollars).

The objective of the brochure is to communicate the benefits of EPR to the market targets (telecine operators and engineers) so they will be prompted to take a buying action.

Notice how the headline and picture work together to (1) hook the reader into turning the page and (2) communicate the benefits of the product. The words "Light Speed" serve to

FRONT COVER

Figure 9-1

INSIDE 1

This product never existed before.

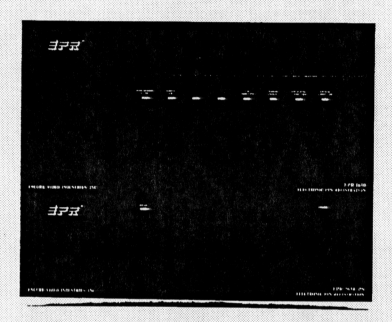

Pin registered film-to-tape transfer has always been a slow, tedious process. Until now.

Pin-registered Transfers in Real Time
The EPR (Electronic Pin Registration) System developed by Encore Video Industries, Inc. (EVI) is a newly-advanced, high-tech means of pin registering film on an EPR-retrofitted Rank Cintel MKIII Telecine. This sys-

tem achieves accurate pin registration in real time without the use of traditional frame-at-a-time mechanical pin intermittent pull-down movements.

The Latest in Optical Technology
Using the latest advances in electro-optical technology, EPR measures and corrects the true horizontal and vertical registration error at an extremely high rate as the film weaves across the gate. In reality, the film still weaves as it passes the gate, but EPR light is now imaging the "perfs" continuously,

detecting every intricate movement and electronically repositioning the Rank picture.

Perfect Registration in Real Time
Since error detection and correction occurs instantaneously, registration is achieved at the Telecine's "real-time" speed of 16 to 30 frames per second. This is from 6 to 30 times faster than mechanical registration systems on the market.

Figure 9-2

INSIDE 2

But the need for it exists every day.

In those cases where non-real time is required, EPR operates in a non-real time mode.

Whatever the speed, the EPR system allows transfer with complete horizontal and vertical repeatability with any number of passes or repetitions.

It Has Nothing to Wear
Because light is used in place of mechanical devices, not only is the registration achieved instantaneously, it also takes place without causing any additional wear on the film. What's more, there are no moving parts in EPR's gate assembly to wear out and cause interruption of the registration process.

But Any Size Will Fit
EPR allows registered transfers in any standard to all video tape formats. By adding the optional FVS 100 sequencer, repeatable film to video field sequencing at all speeds and in all standards can also be achieved.

Easy Installation
The EPR system can be installed by trained technicians in just a couple of days. Using the same Rank lens and with only a couple of retrofitted components to the Rank gate, the EPR *gate* conversion literally takes only 15 minutes or less to complete. In addition, the EPR does not encumber the Rank Cintel in any way. It is a software-based standalone system that operates as an independent unit. It can be turned off and on at the mere "flick of a switch." X and Y positioning, Zoom and all shuttle speeds remain unaffected. What's more, EPR does not require any modifications to the Digiscan, and a Rank CRT Air Knife hook up is provided.

Flexible, Software Based System
Since EPR is a software-based system, it is easy to modify or upgrade your system as enhancements are made. EPR owners can benefit from these improvements by opting to sign up for EPR's Software Maintenance Agreement. For a nominal annual fee, all those who select this option will receive new features and improvements at no additional charge.

Easy to Service
The system's modular design provides the benefit of enabling EVI engineers to easily diagnose problems and send you board replacements if the EPR unit requires service. This swapping of boards minimizes possible "down time" and reduces the costs of servicing the system.

Whatever your needs, our commitment to you goes beyond selling you a system. We are always there for you when you need us.

Remote Control Too
As a convenience, the system comes with a remote control unit that enables you to operate all EPR functions from a remote area.

Let Us Bring You Up to Our Speed
For more information about EPR, please call (213) 466-7663. Or write Encore Video Industries, Inc., 6344 Fountain Avenue, Hollywood, CA 90028.

What's Included
The EPR System includes:
- EPR control unit and power supply unit which come in two separate enclosures for easy rack mounting.
- A remote unit for controlling the system from a remote area.
- Other EPR retrofitting components and interconnecting cables.
- F.O.B. Hollywood, California.
- Installation (not including travel expenses).
- Training.
- Phone support.
- One-year parts and labor warranty.
- System manual/documentation.

Optional Items
- FVS 100 sequencer that offers repeatable film to video frame sequencing at all speeds.
- EVI's annual software maintenance agreement, includes all software upgrades.

Figure 9-3

BACK COVER

Specifications

Line Standard:	525/625 lines, automatically switchable
Power Requirements:	117 VAC / 240 VAC 50Hz / 60Hz
Environmental Characteristics	
Operating Temperature:	10 deg C to 25 deg C
Film Types:	Negative, Interpositive, Color Reversal,
	Intermediate or any similar density base
	surrounding the perf area.
Film Perf Requirements:	4 or 3 Perf 35 mm Bell & Howell Perf
	4 or 3 Perf 35 mm Kodak Perf
Power Consumption	
EPR System:	Less than 100 watts
FVS 100 Sequencer (Optional):	Less than 100 watts
EPR Processor Unit	
Height:	8.75 in (22.23 cm)
Depth:	19.00 in (48.26 cm)
Width:	19.00 in (48.26 cm)
Weight:	30.00 lb (13.64 kg)
EPR Power Supply Unit	
Height:	5.25 in (13.34 cm)
Depth:	19.00 in (48.26 cm)
Width:	19.00 in (48.26 cm)
Weight:	45.00 lb (20.47 kg)
EPR Remote Unit	
Height:	6.00 in (15.24 cm)
Depth:	2.00 in (5.08 cm)
Width:	6.00 in (15.24 cm)
Weight:	2.00 lb (0.91 kg)
FVS 100 Sequencer (Optional)	
Height:	3.50 in (8.89 cm)
Depth:	19.00 in (48.26 cm)
Width:	19.00 in (48.26 cm)
Weight:	10.00 lb (4.55 kg)
Optimum Operating Conditions:	
The distance between the EPR system and the Rank Cintel	
should be no greater than 10 feet (3.05 meters).	
The Remote Unit interconnect should be no greater than	
40 feet (7.62 meters) from the EPR system.	
Specifications are subject to change at any time without notice.	

ENCORE VIDEO
I N D U S T R I E S

6344 Fountain Avenue, Hollywood, CA 90028
213 · 466 · 7643

Figure 9-4

communicate the two primary benefits of the product in a very clever way. Firstly, the two words taken together indicate that the product is very fast. Secondly, the word "Light" is used to convey the idea that light is used in place of mechanical pins. The picture reinforces this notion by showing how light is beamed through the sprocket holes of film. Three layers of film are shown to communicate the use of the product in the compositing of three standard layers of elements — the background, the matte (which is used to cut a whole in the background in the shape of the foreground image) and the foreground. The picture also conveys speed by showing a rocket ship in space as the foreground element. At the same time, it communicates state-of-the art technology — a characteristic of the product and a sub-objective of the brochure's main message (to contrast it from mechanical alternatives). The picture is a photo of an original air-brush painting which the art director commissioned for this brochure. Its originality helps to convey the message that the product is unique. What's more, it's a nice picture.

Product and company identifiers are placed below the picture. Notice how the product name is given top billing over the company name. Also, notice how the company and product names are spelled out using the same typeface as the headline rather than the product and company logos. This is an important point. Amateurish marketers would have chosen the logos. They were not chosen because they would have overwhelmed the graphic focus of the headline and the picture and would have distracted the reader from the more important product messages conveyed by the headline and picture.

In Figure 9-2 and 9-3, the inside story of the brochure unfolds. An inside sub-headline is used to re-inforce the message that the product uses state-of-the-art technology that satisfies an important need.

Between the inside headline and the body text, there is a photo of the product. This photo follows nicely from the introductory words "This product..." in the inside headline.
Boldfaced subheads are used to break up the body text into easy-to-read sections. They reflect the major benefits of the product and flow from one to the other.

Following the guidelines of the UMS, the brochure has a distinctive close punctuated by the sub-headline "Let Us Bring You Up to Our Speed" which ties in nicely with the front cover headline and the main them of the brochure. It also asks the reader to take a buying action (call or write).

A picture of the product in a working setting is used to graphically separate the close from the "What's Included" and "Optional Items" sections.

The back cover contains the product specifications and the logo as a closing signature. The address and phone number is supplied as a convenience for interested prospects to call or write (they don't have to turn back to the Close section).

In general, this brochure is a good example. It follows the guidelines of the UMS. It has a strong hook. It is done in good taste and with some creativity. The overall design and graphics of this brochure was done by Douglas Boyd Design and Marketing, 6624 Melrose Avenue, Los Angeles, CA 90038.

CONCLUSION.

Always remember that the brochure is the center piece of your marketing. More than any other marketing piece, it is the one that represents your company and products. Unlike ads whose messages are short-lived, the brochure, if properly designed, will have a long and prosperous shelf life. It will be handed or sent to people who have already expressed an interest in your products and your company. As such, it should work hard to convince these interested prospects that your product is the one to buy and that your company is the one to buy it from.

To get a good feel for brochures, look at a lot of them — particularly those of your competitors. Don't copy them. Remember, you want yours to stand out rather than be a "me too" document. You want to use them for ideas. You also want to make sure that yours looks at least as good or better (not in your eyes but in the eyes of your prospects and customers).

The next chapter will examine another document that is useful in marketing to your customers and prospects — the Newsletter.

SUGGESTED EXERCISES

1. Collect brochures from each of your main competitors.

2. Collect a brochure (not necessary from your competitors) which you really like. Identify the reasons why you like it on a piece of paper.

3. Ask a couple of market targets or customers what they think of the competitive brochures and the one that you really like. Write down why they like or dislike each one. Particularly note the reasons which don't agree with your own.

4. Using the information collected above, rough out a dummy brochure which you believe will appeal to your target audience.

5. Ask some targets what they think. Note areas of discrepancy, and refine your brochure accordingly.

Notes.

Chapter 10 • NEWSLETTERS

"One of the most effective ways of reaching publics..."

WHAT ARE THEY?

As the name implies, newsletters are a means of providing news about your company and products in a letter style to your various publics. Important publics who should receive newsletters include the following: customers, prospects, employees, prospective employees, past employees, vendors, past vendors, investors, directors, government officials, certain public interest groups, and virtually anyone else with whom your company comes into contact. These groups represent both close and distant parts of your company's family. Including them on your newsletter list is one action which makes them feel as if they are part of the family.

WHY SEND THEM TO ALL PUBLICS?

Some may think that including all your publics on the newsletter mailing list is a bit of overkill and a waste of money. It's not. The reason is that people move in and out of different groups. Someone who is a past employee may become a prospect or customer, or a vendor may become a key employee. Even if members of other publics don't become customers or valued employees, each person with whom your company comes in contact should be looked upon as a potential ambassador, or unpaid sales person, who can positively "spread the word" about your company and products. Developing positive relationships with various publics builds trust and goodwill. Trust and goodwill, in turn, bring referrals and sales.

KEEP CUSTOMERS INFORMED.

In most companies, the best source of referrals and additional sales are existing customers. Because the newsletter can be routinely sent to each and every customer, it is perhaps your company's best and least expensive vehicle for staying "in touch" with all your customers. It is well-suited for telling customers about new products, upgrades, add-ons, specials, operating tips, company achievements, customer testimonials and successes, and any other company news. In addition, it serves to remind customers about your various mainstay products. If they need or want any of them, the newsletter could prompt them to buy.

TAKE NEWSLETTERS SERIOUSLY.

Because of their importance to maintaining good relations, the company should take newsletters seriously and make every effort to do a good job producing them. This means that they should be published at regular intervals. Quarterly is good frequency. Additionally, a talented team of professionals should be given the responsibility of creating them. This team typically includes one or more of the following: an editor, a staff of writers, a photographer, and a graphics person. These can be chosen from the company's pool of talent, outside marketing firms, or a combination of both. Many companies enlist the writing talents of industry executives for their newsletters. These executives are often happy to write articles "free of charge" since it gives them an additional forum for communicating their ideas and for helping to market their own company's products.

DOES NOT REQUIRE A LARGE BUDGET.

It should be mentioned that the newsletter is one of the few marketing pieces that does not need to be receive the "slick" finishing touches of outside professionals. It contains news, and people are familiar with receiving news in black and white on newsprint. Furthermore, with the rapid changes characteristic of most products today, most people prefer timely and accurate news to old "news" which is beautifully presented. In fact, some of the most coveted newsletters are inexpensively-reproduced copies of hand-typed sheets.

With today's desktop publishing systems, you have the best of both worlds. You can report timely news in a good-looking package. In fact, many newsletters produced in this way look as if they have been executed by graphics professionals. If your company does not have and does not want to invest in a desktop publishing system, you can utilize the services of many small firms that specialize in providing inexpensive desktop publishing services. Another alternative is to rent a system whenever you need to use it. If you find that you are paying as much to rent it as it would cost to lease it on a lease/purchase basis, you can always decide to buy one of your own.

NEWSLETTER OBJECTIVES.

The objectives of the newsletter should include one or more of the following:

1. Make publics feel as if they are part of the company family. Most people will do business with people they know and trust before they give their business to strangers.

2. Develop and maintain positive relationships with publics. As described above, positive relationships accelerate sales since they create a network of unpaid ambassadors.

3. Remind customers and other publics of existing products. Many companies fail to realize that customers may not know all the products which they sell. The newsletter is a good place to remind them.

4. Introduce customers and other publics to new products. Customers are perhaps the company's best source of sales for new products. Since they already know the company from previous purchases, they are more apt to purchase new products which they need and/or want.

5. Generate sales to customers and prospects. Since customers already know something about the company and its products, newsletters can prompt quick customer sales. They can also help to convert prospects into customers.

6. Describe new and important uses of existing products. The more uses for a product, the more sales will be made. For example, the makers of *Armoral*, a product used to clean, polish and protect rubber and vinyl in automobiles, found that a good way to increase sales is to show customers how the product can do the same for patio furniture and other household vinyl products.

7. Explain techniques for accomplishing various tasks using company products. Helping customers to use the product serves two important purposes — (1) It shows that the company is customer oriented which strengthens the bond between company and customer which, in turn, promotes free positive "word of mouth" advertising; and (2) It creates additional uses as described in #6 above.

8. Provide customer case histories and success stories. Providing prospects and customers with other success stories serves to make them more comfortable with the company and products. People buy more from companies with which they are comfortable.

9. Bring company news to publics. Company news keeps the publics informed and makes them feel part of the company.

10. Demonstrate that the company is interested in providing on-going service to customers. Many customers never hear from companies after they buy their products. Receiving the company's newsletter continues the relationship. It communicates to customers and prospects that the company is interested in servicing its customers.

11. Provide company publics with industry trends. Since their businesses often depend on industry trends, they appreciate receiving such information.

12. Communicate company and product benefits. Unlike print ads and brochures, newsletters don't have to be formal or general. They can informally communicate benefits in the context of useful tips and specific customer case histories. Because they are less of an overt selling piece than other forms of marketing, they are often more effective at communicating these benefits.

13. Position the company relative to the competition. Newsletters provide the space and proper context for comparing the company and its products to the competition. As with other forms of marketing, however, they should avoid "bad-mouthing" the competition.

14. Give recognition to employees. Employees who work hard to make your company successful can be featured in newsletters via publications of awards, honors and feature articles.

CHARACTERISTICS.

To achieve the objectives set forth above, newsletters should have certain inherent characteristics. They should be:

- **Newsworthy.** It's more important to get the newsletter out on a timely basis than to present a slick piece with old news.

- **Informative.** In addition to providing news about the company picnic, it should contain information that will be useful to most customers such as helpful hints in using company products, new product information, and customer case histories.

- **Informal.** It should be "folksy" and casual. It should use colorful, conversational language rather than dry, formal sentences.

- **Personal.** It should talk "one on one" to each person in the audience. For example, use of the personal pronoun "you" is recommended over more impersonal language such as "one" or "most people".

- **Friendly.** It should have a friendly attitude. Again the idea is communicating with friends and members of the company's immediate family.

- **Professional.** Although informal and personal, it should be professional at the same time. No street language or offensive slang. No "put downs", negatives or other no no's.

- **Follow the Rules.** As discussed in previous sections, the newsletter should follow the concepts and structures of good marketing principles and the UMS.

WHAT SHOULD THEY CONTAIN?

A well-constructed newsletter usually contains several sections.

Cover

On the cover are several different elements including the following:

Title. Every newsletter should have a title. It could simply be the company name followed by the word "NEWS" or "REPORT"; or it could be a given name that somehow relates to the company's products. For example, a company in Denver, Colorado named Technical Information Associates, Inc. which offers consulting services under the name "The Mentor Series" uses the name "Docu-MENTOR" for its newsletter. A small insurance firm that goes by the name of the President, Elliot V. Matloff, uses "EVM NEWS" as the title of its newsletter.

If the company name is used in the title, it may or may not be used in conjunction with the company logo.

Descriptive Phrase. Following the Title (with or without company logo), many newsletters use a phrase to describe the newsletter. Examples include: "A publication of XYZ Corporation"; "The Newsletter for Seminar Alumni"; "A Resource for Successful Corporate Video Communication"; "A quarterly publication of ABC Corp., developers of the X-line of products".

Company Identifier. If the company is not identified in either the Title or the Descriptive Phrase, it should appear somewhere else on the cover page (usually on the top or bottom in the form of the name and/or logo). You want to make sure that readers know that the newsletter is from your company. There are no advantages and only disadvantages from keeping them guessing.

Issue Identifier. After the title and descriptive phrase, there is an issue identifier which specifies the particular issue according some logical sequence. This usually takes the form of a Date and/or a Volume and Sequence number. For example, if the newsletter is issued quarterly and is in its fourth year of publication, the Summer Issue might be identified as follows: "Summer 1989", or "Volume 4 No. 3" (assuming the series number begins in the Winter as No. 1), or both. While some newsletters use one or the other, most newsletters use both. The only reason not to use both is if the newsletter does not come out regularly, or the company is a new company that does not want to remind its customers that it is in its first or second year of existence. If properly marketed, however, the newness of a company can be turned into an advantage rather than a liability.

Table of Contents. On the cover of some newsletters, nestled amidst the cover story body text, is a quasi-Table of Contents which summarizes the important features contained in the newsletter. This Table of Contents often appears in a box or is sectioned off from the other portions of the cover by horizontal lines and is headlined by the phrase such as, "In this issue... ". Each featured section is typically highlighted with a bullet, a hand, or some other symbol.

Cover Story. Most newsletters have one or more cover stories that begin on the front page. These articles typically follow the UMS with a catchy headline, boldfaced subheads, close, etc. The Lead Story (or first article) is usually the most important one or the one which will attract the most attention and get the reader interested in turning the page to read other items of interest.

Picture or Graphic. The front page usually has a picture or graphic relating to the subject of the Lead Story or the author.

This picture serves to attract attention, to reinforce the text and to graphically break up the text and make it more inviting to read. Unless it is very newsworthy, the cover picture and story should have more substance than the company picnic or baseball game. While these might be interesting for certain publics, customers and prospects are less likely to be motivated to continue reading with this type of lead. Pictures and accompanying stories about new products or new uses of existing products are likely to attract more interest and generate more sales.

Special Items. There are times when you want to highlight a special item or special offer that is contained on the inside pages of the newsletter. While you can't put it on the front cover for some reason, you can put a *teaser* or *flag* on the front cover that readers are sure to see. This purpose of this flag is to encourage readers to turn to the special item of interest. There are several techniques for doing this. One is to put the teaser in the upper or lower right corner of the cover at a 45-degree angle. Another is to use a shade of color or tone which distinguishes the flagged item from the remainder of the text. Still another is to highlight the teaser by presenting it over a contrasting background of color or tone. To insure readers will see it, some newsletters use a combination of the above techniques — i.e. a corner of the newsletter is shaded red and the special item teaser is printed in white at a 45-degree angle. The teaser might say something such as, "FREE SEMINAR WINNERS INSIDE" or "FREE COMPUTER SOFTWARE... DETAILS INSIDE."

Price. Many newsletters are sold to subscribers. Even if they are not, some believe it is a good idea to put a price on the front cover of the newsletter near the Sequence Identifier. The reason is that people will appreciate it more if it has a tangible value. Often times, even if the newsletter is sold to certain subscribers, it is given to customers and prospects at no charge.

Inside Pages

More of the Same. The inside pages of most newsletters typically contain a continuation of the cover articles, more stories, more pictures, graphs, charts, product and price information, special offers, ... you name it. Since the inside pages often cover very important and useful information, it's a good idea to make sure each one has a "catchy" headline to draw the reader's attention.

Ads.   To help finance the cost of their newsletters, some companies and organizations may sell ad space to selected advertisers (competitors are to be avoided). Some also provide this ad space free of charge to selected customers. While some believe ads "cheapen" the newsletter, others feel it provides a useful service to both customers and advertisers. It certainly doesn't hurt the image of magazines or directories. Moreover, the content and quality of the newsletter is more likely to affect image than the inclusion of ads.

Product and Price Summary.   If feasible, a summary of the company's products and services along with prices should be included in each newsletter. If there are too many of these to include, information on how the reader can obtain such a summary should be provided instead. After all, the newsletter presents a terrific low-key and low-cost opportunity to sell company products to its most qualified prospects — existing customers. This opportunity should not be lost.

Feedback Form.   Some of the most valuable market research comes from customers. The newsletter provides an unbelievable opportunity to obtain such research. Each newsletter should have a Feedback Form similar to the one shown in *Figure 10-1*. Customers should be encouraged to voice their suggestions, complaints and compliments on this form.

Information from suggestions and complaints should go to the appropriate marketing, engineering, and product development people. Marketing should review compliments for possible use in testimonial ads, case histories, and other company marketing. Even if not used in marketing pieces, copies of the compliments should be circulated to sales and marketing people for inclusion in their sales presentation notebooks. Copies should be also circulated to all company offices for incorporation in a "Publicity Book" that is kept in the lobby so that visitors can read about company successes while they are waiting for appointments.

FEEDBACK FORM.

Although we believe our products to be amongst the very best, we want to continually improve them to meet your changing needs. In order to do this, we need your help. We would like to know what you think of our products. Your responses will enable us to channel our resources in the proper direction. Please feel free to say anything you like below or on an attached piece of paper.

Thank you for taking your time to provide us with this information. We want you to know how much we appreciate your business. When convenient, please return this form to XYZ Corp., 2222 C Street, Anywhere, CA 99999. Postage is prepaid for your convenience.

Figure 10-1

Return Coupon/Order Form. Every newsletter should contain either a return coupon or order form which makes it easy for readers to order products or request more information. The easier you make it for the customer to order or obtain information on products, the more products you will sell. This coupon or order form should be coded so that you know the exact issue or source from which it came. Some people hold on to these for a long time before sending them in. In these cases, they can overlap with more current coupons and order forms. The reason for coding is so you can measure the effectiveness of each newsletter and you can compare it with the cost effectiveness of other marketing pieces and promotional strategies.

Distribution. The newsletter should list the various locations where customers and prospects can buy the company's products. This includes name (if it's a dealer or distributor outside the company), address, phone number, and (if appropriate) fax number.

Other Items. In addition to the above, the newsletter may or may not contain the following: schedule of upcoming events, awards, regular columns that appear in each issue, messages from the president or other top executives, promotions and discounts specially offered to readers, important date reminders, helpful tips on using products, new uses for existing products, questionnaires, and a variety of other items.

Back Cover

As with the back cover of all marketing pieces, the back cover of the newsletter is very important. Depending on the style of the newsletter and how it is mailed it will most likely contain one or more of the following:

Mailing Information. Since many newsletters are designed to serve as self-mailers, the back cover is typically reserved for special mailing purposes. Usually it's designed so that the newsletter can be folded, affixed with a mailing label, and sent to prospective readers. In such cases, it should have the company's return address printed on it. It's also not a bad idea to have the main company phone number printed below the return address for the reader's convenience. At the bottom of the side that contains the mailing label, it should have a forwarding notice such as "Address Correction Requested", "Forwarding and Return Postage Guaranteed", or "Please Forward". To avoid having to hand stamp every newsletter, it's also a good idea to have a "Bulk Rate U.S. Postage PAID Permit" pre-printed in the upper right corner of the mailing section (where a postage stamp would go). If there's a choice, it's even more important to have a Postage PAID permit on the back of coupons or order forms which you want readers to return.

Continuation of Inside Pages. In those cases where the newsletter will me mailed in a business envelope, the back page can be a continuation of the inside pages.

Other Items. If not devoted entirely to out-going mailing information, the back cover often contains return coupons, order forms, or distribution locations. Also, if not already included on the inside pages, the back cover may contain a closing paragraph which instructs readers what to do if they wish additional information.

Logo/Closing Signature. Whether it appears on the front cover or not, the back cover should contain the company logo as part of the closing signature. A company or product slogan may also be part of the signature.

General Newsletter Items. In addition to the above, a well-prepared newsletter should contain the following additional items: page numbers, one or two colors, and coordinated type styles. A mistake too often made by companies is the use of too many different type styles and sizes in their newsletters. This makes the newsletter look amateurish. The newsletter should be limited to variations (standard, italic and boldface) on one or two type faces.

MAILING LIST.

As with any marketing piece that is routinely mailed, it is very important to properly maintain the mailing list of your various publics. What does maintaining your mailing list mean? It means adding new prospects, customers, and members of other publics on a timely basis (If you don't, they will not receive important mailings). It means including a forwarding message as discussed above. It also means keep track of all returned newsletters and making name, title, and address changes to your mailing list as you learn of them. Maintaining a mailing list is one of the most tedious and least desirable activities in business. On an enjoyment level, it ranks somewhere between preparing tax returns and searching for documents which you've misfiled. It is essential, however for a number of reasons. It provides you with valuable information about your various publics. It avoids your wasting money on postage and newsletters sent to wrong people and places. Moreover, it avoids angering or embarrassing recipients via misspelling their names, misidentifying their genders or positions, or repeatedly sending their mail to the wrong address.

NEWSLETTER EXAMPLE.

To illustrate the application of some of the points discussed above, it is useful to look at an actual newsletter. The example selected is from a consulting firm named Kalb & Associates, which happens to be the author's consulting firm. As shown in *Figure 10-2* (A through D), this is an example of a newsletter that is very inexpensively produced on a computer with word processing and desktop publishing capabilities and reprinted at a local, low-cost printer. This example was selected to illustrate how an inexpensive newsletter format can be effective. As discussed earlier, the newsletter is perhaps the only marketing piece in which the timeliness of the news and the clarity of presentation is more important than the "slickness" of the piece. Some of the most effective and popular newsletters sold by subscription are mimeographed copies of typewritten sheets. It should be noted, however, that if you are going to use an inexpensive format, it's a good idea to explain why in the first newsletter of the series. For example, one firm named EVI explained in Volume 1 No. 1 the reason for its format as follows:

"The style of this Newsletter will be informal and non-commercial so as to hold down the costs and to provide timely information that is still newsworthy. As you know, 'slick' newsletters are costly, and such

Newsletter Front Cover

K&A NEWS

A Special Information Resource for Clients, Friends, and Associates of KALB & ASSOCIATES • K&A PRESS

Fall/Winter 1991   **Volume 5 Number 1 $10**

 ## Recession Marketing

At the first signs of recession, many companies follow a cost cutting strategy which they believe will balance costs with projected lower revenues. While this makes logical sense to some, it is simply the wrong strategy.

In a recessionary economy, you need to do more marketing — not less. Yes, while it may seem counter-intuitive, you need to do more marketing to generate business when business slows down. Doing less marketing in a recession is similar to turning up the heat when it's hot, or turning on the air conditioning when it's cold. You need to do those *things* which will turn the current situation around — i.e. create more business opportunities, build more relationships with customers, and get your message into more people's minds. If you do less, you are likely to accelerate the downturn in business or, if you're lucky, maintain the less-than-satisfactory status quo.

Doing more does not necessarily mean spending more. While most companies cut their marketing activities in a downturn as a reflex action, they should know that doing more and spending less don't have to be mutually exclusive. That is, if you

> Doing less marketing in a recession is similar to turning up the heat when it's hot, or turning on the air conditioning when it's cold.

really know what you're doing, you can do more without increasing the marketing budget. In fact, in many cases, you can actually do more and spend less.

Doing more for less. How can you do more marketing for less money? In general, you need to do the following: (1) Better target your customers, (2) Clearly position your products and your company in the minds of those targets, and (3) Substitute more expensive with less expensive forms of marketing.

Better Targeting your customers. In a downturn, you need to identify those prospects who are most likely to buy your products. While this may require a little homework, it is something you should do irrespective of the state of the economy. In fact, doing a better job of identifying your market targets does not have to be expensive or time consuming. In the absence of doing sophisticated research, you can simply identify the common char-

Please see Recession Marketing Page 2.

 ## Happy Holidays

All of us at Kalb & Associates and K&A press would like to wish you and your associates a Merry Christmas, a Happy Hanukkah, and the happiest, healthiest, and most prosperous of New Years.

 ## K&A on TV Show

Ira Kalb recently appeared as a panelist on *Third Thursday,* an award-winning talk show hosted by the NBC news anchor, Marty Levin. The subject of the show was *Multi-level marketing,* and Mr. Kalb was asked to add the marketing perspective to the panel which included the Deputy Attorney General of the State of California, an attorney who represents several multi-level marketing firms, and a representative of the Small Business Administration.

Inside Contents

Figure 10-2A

Newsletter Inside Pages 1

Recession Marketing   Continued from Page 1

acteristics of existing customers and find and reach prospects with the same characteristics. To find them, you should again turn to existing customers. You can identify the publications they read. By doing this, you are likely to discover key industry publications which are effective vehicles for reaching them. Moreover, many companies find that advertising in these industry publications is often less expensive and more effective for reaching market targets than existing advertising vehicles. Such publications typically maintain demographic data on their readership which allows you to confirm their efficiency at reaching your targets.

Better Positioning. Once you identify your most promising targets, you need to make sure that you clearly *position* your products and your company in the minds of these targets. In its simplest form, positioning involves letting your prospects *know what business you are in.* In more competitive markets, you should also clearly communicate the *unique advantages and benefits* of your products and company over those of your competitors.

Substitute less expensive forms of marketing. In addition to doing better targeting and positioning, a company can afford to do more marketing in a recession if they substitute less expensive marketing methods. For example, instead of doing color ads, brochures, and mailings, your company can substitute black and white. In fact, for many high-tech and "arty" products, black and white can be just as effective, and a lot less expensive. Instead of having mega-booths at a few trade shows, the company can substitute smaller booths, and perhaps attend more shows. Rather than attend certain shows, your company might consider inviting show attendees to a seminar held at your local office or in a hotel suite near the show site. In this way, you can effectively reach show attendees without incurring large booth expenses and the noise and competitive distractions of the show floor. Instead of incurring the expense of calling on customers directly, you can make more frequent contacts via outbound telemarketing, faxes, and personal letters. In lieu of putting a few full-page ads in expensive general media, you can place more ads in less-expensive industry publications and more closely-targeted media.

Increase the use of "Free" marketing vehicles. In addition to using *lower-cost* marketing methods, you can intensify your use of *"no-cost"* marketing.

No cost marketing involves such techniques as the following: (1) Maintaining good relationships with targeted media and sending them regular press releases on your products and accomplishments, (2) Encouraging good writers in your company to write articles about your products and to submit them to the above targeted media, (3) Spoiling your customers so that they will be prompted to spread the positive word about your company and products, (4) Enlisting the help of all your publics to help you sell your products to the marketplace.

Helping your sales force to be more efficient. One of the most effective ways of increasing your marketing efforts without significantly increasing your marketing budget is to improve the efficiency of your sales force. This involves providing your sales force with information which (1) documents the advantages of your products and services over those of your competitors, (2) delineates the deficiencies of your competitors, (3) describes the successes your customers have achieved from using your products and services, and (4) provides independent third-party validation of your company's successes and accomplishments.

Creating and Implementing an effective marketing information system. Providing the above information to the sales force typically involves creating a *marketing information system* which collects and distributes this information to sales personnel on a timely basis. Such a system does not have to be complex or costly to implement. Some companies have been successfully using a very simplified version which merely collects and reports (1) comments from customers, prospects, vendors, and other publics, (2) articles published in important media, and (3) information collected at trade shows, industry conferences and other important forums. Once established, this same marketing information system can also be used to collect and report valuable information on new opportunities in the marketplace, new product ideas, feedback on the performance of your marketing strategies, and suggestions for improving your products and services.

Summary. The above techniques should provide you with some good ideas for doing more marketing on a static or even shrinking marketing budget. The important point to remember is that when there is a business downturn, you need to do more marketing — not less.

Figure 10-2B

Newsletter Inside Pages 2

 KALB & ASSOCIATES SEMINARS

In addition to our consulting services, Kalb & Associates continues to offer business seminars such as those listed below:

High-tech Marketing. This is a marketing course which is designed for both beginning and seasoned marketers. It is recommended for all those who either have marketing responsibilities or who deal with the public.

Selling High-tech Products and Services. This is an intensive course aimed at teaching sales fundamentals and practical techniques to beginning as well as veteran sales professionals.

Creating Ads and Promotional Programs. This course focuses on helping marketing students and professionals to develop actual ads and marketing programs for their companies and organizations.

Structuring Your Company for Greater Success. This is an important course for anyone needing to develop systems to properly organize the company and its departments.

Marketing to Europe: The Challenge of 1992. This is a travel study course centered in London which is designed to help marketing executives to successfully penetrate the unified European market of 1992.

Sales Force Management. This course trains sales and marketing personnel to be competent sales force managers.

Advertising and Promotion Management. This course trains marketing personnel to properly manage the advertising and promotion functions of an organization.

Customer Service: A Powerful Competitive Strategy. This course trains managers and employees alike how to deliver improved customer service which will greatly benefit the company's bottom line.

Marketing Information System: A key Ingredient for Success. This course teaches marketing personnel to create and utilize a marketing information system to benefit the company and its publics.

 BOOKS K&A PRESS

If you are unable to attend K&A Seminars but would like to purchase the texts used in these courses, you may order the following books from K&A Press for $39.95 plus tax, shipping and handling: *High-tech Marketing: A Practical Approach; Creating Your Own Marketing Makes Good $ and Sense; Selling High-tech Products and Services,* K&A Press, 1991. They are also often available at the *LuValle Commons* bookstore on the UCLA campus, Tams at USC or the *OPAMP* Bookstore in Hollywood. Clients and students of Kalb & Associates may purchase them directly from the publisher at a discounted price of $34.95 plus tax. With shipping and handling, the price would be $39.95 in the United States and $49.95 overseas. If you are interested in ordering one or more of these books, please complete and send in the information form at the end of this newsletter, or call 310•829-9790.

 MOST RECENT K&A ENGAGEMENTS

To give you a better understanding of the scope of the services we offer, we have described some of our most recent client engagements below.

Marketing Plan. We recently developed and revised a marketing plan for a high-tech firm which make communications secure products for satellites.

Business Plans. We created business plans for firms which specialize in the digital signal processing, import/export, and cable TV industries.

Publicity. We wrote an article to give publicity to a firm in the television industry.

Advertising and promotion strategies. We developed an advertising and promotion strategies for a small start-up firm in the food in beverage industry, and for a major university.

Brochures. We designed and developed a brochure for a high-technology start-up.

Distribution Strategy. We created a distribution strategy for a well-known international firm in the entertainment industry.

Marketing Programs. We developed marketing programs for a book publisher.

Positioning Strategy. We developed a positioning strategy (including name and logo) for a start-up software company.

Systems. We helped a large software company to select and install an accounting system.

These recent engagements are representative of just some of the marketing, sales, business systems, and management consulting services which we offer to our clients. If you have any consulting needs, please do not hesitate to call us to discuss our capabilities for servicing them. Because of the *unique* way we are structured we have associates that can help you with virtually every aspect of your business.

We hope to be speaking or meeting with you very soon. In the interim, if you have any questions, please do not hesitate to call us at your convenience.

Figure 10-2C

Newsletter Back Cover

Address Correction Requested
Please Forward

KALB & ASSOCIATES
2618 Montana Avenue, Suite #1
Santa Monica, CA 90403

For more information on our consulting services, seminars, or books please call **310•829-9790** or write to **Kalb & Associates, 2618 Montana Avenue, Suite 1, Santa Monica, CA 90403**. If more convenient, please complete and send us the information below.

Name: _____

Position: _____

Company: _____

Street: _____

City, ST, Zip: _____

Phone: _____

Please Indicate Your Interest Below.   12/0891
☐ CONSULTING: _____
☐ BOOKS: ☐ High-tech Marketing; ☐ Creating Your Own Marketing Makes Good $ and Sense; ☐ High-tech Selling.
☐ SEMINARS: ☐ High-tech Marketing; ☐ Selling High-tech Products; ☐ Creating Promotional Programs; ☐ Structuring Your Business for Success; ☐ Marketing to Europe: 1992; ☐ Customer Service; ☐ Marketing Information System.
☐ OTHER: _____

MARKETING TIP

You can determine if you have a good positioning strategy by simply asking your customers, "What image does are products bring to mind?" If they all give you similar answers, you know your strategy is working. If they don't, you have a positioning problem. If you find that your position is not clear, there is a bright side. You can make it clear and improve your sales. For example, most people know Volvo's position — safety, and Maytag's — reliability. What is Chevrolet's?

K&A NEWS is published twice yearly by K&A Press, 2618 Montana Avenue, Suite #1, Santa Monica, CA 90403, 310•829-9790. If any of your associates would like to receive this newsletter, please let us know, and we will be happy to add them to our mailing list.

© 1991 K&A PRESS. All rights reserved.

Figure 10-2D

costs typically get passed on to customers. More importantly, they often have 'old news' since the lead times for typesetting, proofing, and printing can be rather long. To avoid these problems, EVI's newsletter will be generated on our own word processors, printed on our laser printer, and copied at our local printers."

Getting back to our example, you can see that the Newsletter has a title formed by the name of the firm followed by the word "NEWS". This is followed by a statement which describes the intended audience. A line is used to separate this *title section* from the issue identifier.

In the *issue identifier,* this firm decided to use both a seasonal reference and a Volume/Number sequencing system. A line is used to separate this section from the main body text. This newsletter does use a *table of contents* in the lower left corner. Note that there is a *lead story* which is continued on inside pages. This allows other important stories to be introduced on the front page. The lead story and other lengthy sections have boldfaced sub-headlines which are concise, to the point, and break up the text into manageable "bite-sized" pieces. The inside pages have a good mix of articles, product information, and other information that might be useful to the firm's audience. The firm's most recent work is summarized according to specific categories to give prospective clients an idea of the kind of work the firm can do for them. There is a distinctive close on the return coupon on the last page. It is coded so the source of returned coupons can be quickly and easily determined. The last page is also designed so that the newsletter can be folded in half, affixed with a stamp and used as a self-mailer.

While this newsletter is not "fancy" it is clear, concise and straightforward. It gets the job done which making a positive impression.

SUMMARY.

In summary, newsletters are an effective and inexpensive means for a company to "stay in touch" with its various publics — especially its customers. They should come out regularly, with quarterly being a good frequency. If done properly that can be extremely effective in selling company products to customers.

SELECTED EXERCISES.

1. Collect three company newsletters from various companies. It would be a good idea if they are in your industry.

2. Write down the various sections in these newsletters on a piece of paper (refer to the "WHAT SHOULD THEY CONTAIN? " Section above if necessary).

3. Star the sections that are common to all three.

4. Write down what you particularly like about each of these newsletters.

5. Compose a newsletter for your organization based on what you did in items #2 through #4 above.

Notes.

Chapter 11 • SEMINARS & TRADE SHOWS

"One-on-many is a very efficient way to sell"

WHAT ARE SEMINARS?

Seminars are scheduled meetings in which a group of people with similar interests are brought together to learn about a particular subject matter.   In the context of a company's promotional efforts, they are often used as an effective way of marketing products.

The reason prospects are attracted to seminars is that it affords them an opportunity to learn more about a company, product or a technology in which they have an interest, and they can do so with anonymity.   That is, they don't feel the pressure or obligation often associated with a one-on-one sales presentation. They can listen to the seminar presenter as an anonymous observer in a crowd of people. If they want to leave, they can do so (in most cases) without embarrassment or without interrupting the presentation.

As for the company, it gives them the opportunity to reach many prospects with one well-honed presentation.

Because seminars are educational in orientation, they are an excellent way to market high-tech products and services.

WHY THEY WORK SO WELL.

Unlike printed marketing pieces, marketing via seminars provides the opportunity for face-to-face contact between company personnel and target prospects. In addition to communicating product benefits and features, this forum allows for (1) questions to be asked by prospects and answered by marketing personnel; (2) prospects to see, hear and touch products under "live" conditions; and (3) company personnel to develop those necessary personal relationships with prospective customers.

If done properly, seminars also provide an excellent forum for:

- Educating prospects on the features and benefits of the company's products.

- Tailoring a program to address the specific needs of a particular target market segment.

- Providing an opportunity for one skilled presenter to sell to, or dazzle, many prospects at one time.

- Giving the presenter sufficient time to tell the company's story.

- Soliciting testimonial references from happy customers.

- Attracting qualified prospects (if they take time from their busy schedule to attend the seminar, they are most likely very interested).

- Selling prospective employees and other publics on the company and its products.

Moreover, seminars can usually accomplish the above with a very low budget.

WHAT IS MARKETING'S ROLE?

In most cases, Marketing plays a major role in preparing for, presenting, and following-up on the results of the seminar. For best results, marketers work closely with sales personnel to insure that all aspects of the seminar are well-coordinated and well-presented. There are a lot of important details to be worked out. In particular, marketing and sales need to cooperate to properly plan for, execute, and follow-up on the activity generated by the seminar.

SEMINAR PREPARATION.

To help insure the success of the seminar, careful planning and preparation should be employed. The movie *Wall Street* borrowed an appropriate quote from a book entitled The *Art of War* by a Chinese philosopher named *Sun Tsu.* It goes something like this, "all battles are won before they are fought." While this could apply to planning virtually every aspect of business, it is particularly appropriate in preparing for seminars. The sequence of steps listed below should serve as a useful guide for marketers to follow in preparing for a seminar.

Select the Seminar Topic

The topic should be selected and positioned so as to generate sufficient interest and attendance. It should be aimed at a specific target audience rather than a general audience. For example, a seminar for attorneys, doctors, consultants, retailers, ad agencies or light manufacturers is considerably more effective than a seminar for businesses in general.

Select a Date and Time

Date: The seminar should be scheduled at a date and time which is most convenient for the target prospects. Care should be given to select a date which does not conflict with holidays, trade shows, fiscal year end closings, or normal "days off" for target prospects. For example, Wednesdays are bad for doctors because many take the day off.

Duration: Shorter duration seminars are often more effective than seminars that take all day. Firstly, it's difficult for most prospects to commit time to sitting in a seminar all day. Secondly, most people get restless after an hour or two (remember most movies are cut to between 90 and 120 minutes for that reason). Thirdly, prospects prefer a focused and concise presentation to one which takes all day (but which could have been done within two hours).

Day of Week: Seminars should avoid Mondays and Fridays. Mondays are important "getting started" or "recovering from weekend" days. Moreover, many people tend to be in bad moods on Monday — hardly a time to interest prospects in your products. Friday is the beginning of the weekend so many people have their minds on weekend plans and would have a difficult time concentrating on seminar presentations. This leaves days in the middle of the week — Tuesday, Wednesday and Thursday. Assuming it doesn't conflict with special industry meetings, Tuesday is probably best because prospects are less likely to schedule social plans that evening than on Wednesday or Thursday evening. Also, it gives three more days during the week for sales personnel to follow up on the interests generated in the seminar and to keep them "hot". This is essential because weekends have a tendency to "cool prospects off" and wipe memories clean from the previous week.

Time: The best time for short duration seminars is late afternoon or early evening before dinner. During this time period, the prospect misses the least amount of productive work time, and does not have to miss dinner. Depending on traffic patterns or other factors, another time might be more appropriate. Some companies offer two or three sessions on the same day so prospects can select the time which is most convenient. For example, if you could have two sessions, you could schedule Session 1 from 9 a.m. to 12 noon or 10 a.m. to 1 p.m. and Session 2 from 1 to 4 p.m. or 2 to 5 p.m. (again depending on the specific situation). These staggered times, however, only make sense if you have enough prospects signed up to fill all sessions. It's not a good idea to present a seminar to a half-filled room.

Leveraging other events: Seminars that are targeted to attract prospects from around the world are often held in conjunction with trade shows (i.e. after the normal hours of the show). In this way, they can benefit from prospects who are already coming into town to see the trade show. Because they can leverage their attendance off of the trade show traffic, they are more likely to attract out-of-town prospects who would otherwise find it difficult to make a special trip just to attend the seminar.

Select a Location

If your company's offices are attractive and convenient, they are one of the best (and certainly least expensive) locations — particularly if you are selling products which are not easy to transport. In your offices, you are on your own "turf". You know where everything is located. You know how to "get around" problems that arise; and you have support and service people readily available if any equipment should malfunction during the seminar.

If offices are not attractive and convenient, you might want to consider renting a banquet room at a hotel which is. Depending on the geographical spread of prospects' offices, good locations are usually near airports, freeway intersections, and any other known and easily accessible landmarks. Again, traffic patterns should also be considered when making the selection and setting the times.

In some cases (usually in far off or remote areas), a good location strategy is to hold the seminar at the "nicely appointed" offices of a happy customer. The customer can serve as a testimonial for your product and can show the seminar attendees how he/she is actually using the product. However, you should be sensitive to any competitive problems that this might create between different prospects. In some industries, competitors do not feel comfortable visiting other competitors. Also, the hosting customer may not want competitors wandering around his/her facility.

Creating Invitations

Once all the details of subject, time and location are determined, you should create the invitations and have them printed. Engraved or printed invitations on quality "invitation-style" panel cards are most effective. Some companies are finding even greater success with a new technique — that of printing invitations on post-cards which have an attractive picture on the other side. They claim that, with an attractive post card, prospects are more likely to attend and less likely to throw away the card — even after the event has been held. A pre-test or phone survey of your customer base is recommended before you decide to use post cards.

Invitations should contain the pertinent information: subject, date, time location, information about food and drink that will be served, and instructions to R.S.V.P. to a specific person and phone number by a specific date. Any parking, elevator, or other special instructions should be enclosed with (but probably not included on) the invitation.

While invitations don't often begin with a headline and a hook, they usually have a hook somewhere in the invitation. Getting prospects to attend is no easy task. Giving them a compelling or interesting reason for attending, such as an exciting or well-known speaker or topic, will greatly boost their interest. For emphasis, this compelling reason can be communicated in a slightly larger boldfaced type.

Figure 11-1 shows an example of an actual invitation that was used for a seminar. This invitation has a hook but it's in the close section (or last line) since the company decided not to use a formal headline.

Food and Drink

Arrangements should be made in accordance with caterer (or employee) lead times for food and drink. Lavish, expensive food is not required for a successful seminar. Fruit, cheese, crackers, wine, coffee and tea are usually sufficient and easier to prepare — especially for late afternoon meetings.

Selecting or acquiring the Mailing List

Seminars are most effective if invitees are comprised of prospects who have already had some contact with your company. If this is the case, you will most likely have these prospects already on your mailing list. All that is required is for you to sort your mailing list so that those who would have an interest in the seminar topic are selected.

If you don't already have sufficient prospects on your in-house mailing list, you may need add to this list by purchasing or renting one that is commercially available. You should do some

INVITATION

Encore Video Industries cordially invites you and your associates to a special reception and demonstration of our EPR™ Electronic Pin Registration system during your visit to Los Angeles for the SMPTE show.

We will be hosting demonstrations every hour from 6 p.m. to 10 p.m. each evening of the show (October 30 thru November 4, 1987) at Encore Video's facility located at 6344 Fountain Avenue (between Cahuenga and Vine), Hollywood, CA 90028.

Wine and hors d'oeuvres will be served.

Please call Encore at 213-466-4693 to reserve space at one of these' demonstrations.

Don't miss an opportunity to see for yourself why the whole industry is excited about the real-time registation capabilities of EPR.

Figure 11-1

informal market research to find out which mailing lists are the best for reaching prospects in the target audience of the seminar.

Mailing

Invitations should be mailed so that they arrive on the desk of the prospects no later than two weeks before the date of the seminar, with three weeks being preferable in some circumstances. This means that they should be mailed no later than three weeks before the date of the seminar. Less than two weeks notice creates calendar conflicts, much more than two weeks increases the likelihood that prospects will forget about the seminar. Whenever possible, stamps should be affixed to the envelopes. Secretaries are more likely to forward stamped envelopes than those that have the "mass-produced" look of bulk mail, although a stamp machine is an acceptable alternative in most cases.

RSVP

Instructions to RSVP are important. If food is being served, the instruction should ask for an RSVP no later than a week in advance of the seminar. For smaller-sized seminars, it is best to have prospects RSVP to a specific person and phone number. In addition to making the process more personal, that person can better maintain an accurate list of prospects who've responded. The responder's name, company name and phone number should be recorded on the list. If you have a multi-user computer system which various people in your company can access, RSVPs can be taken by more than one person if necessary. This, of course, is necessary for handling high volumes of RSVPs.

Information Packets

The marketing department should decide what materials are to be handed out at the seminar. After preparing a sample information packet. Marketing should instruct the sales people who will be on duty at the seminar to put the packets together for the attendees. While some may feel that this is a waste of sales people's time, it isn't. It gives them the opportunity to familiarize themselves with the information that will be handed out so that they can prepare themselves to talk intelligently with seminar attendees about this information. Too often, sales personnel don't see this material until just before the seminar. This sometimes leaves them unprepared and embarrassed when they can't answer questions posed by attendees. Typical information packets may or may not include the following:

- Outline of the seminar presentation.
- Background and history information on the company.
- Product line information.
- Brochures on products specifically related to the seminar topic.
- Product specification sheets.
- Customer case histories.
- Price lists (if appropriate).
- Company newsletter.
- Company promotional items, such as pens and pencils.
- Thank you note for attending.

If the company has developed a brochure with a flap or pocket that is appropriate for the seminar, it can be used to neatly contain much of the other information listed above. If not, many companies use folders or large envelopes with their names discreetly printed on them. If the seminar presentation has a special name, it is a good idea to have envelopes or folders printed with this special name on the covers. With a desktop publishing system, this can be done quite easily and inexpensively. Another "nice touch" is to have each prospective attendee's name also printed on the cover. It communicates to them that you are organized and prepared and that you are interested in developing a personal relationship with them.

Seminar Presentation Materials

Marketing is the most qualified group for selecting the materials and writing the basic script of the seminar presentation. Many seminars involve showing films, videos or slides. Sufficient lead time should be allowed to order or prepare these materials and work them into the script of the presentation.

If you have a computer with desktop publishing or presentation capabilities, you can create very sophisticated slides for your presentation. You can even hook your computer system directly into your projectors for "real-time" display of your presentation materials.

Writing boards should be stocked with plenty of markers or chalk. Flip charts should have extra markers. Overhead projectors should have a spare bulb handy. Slide projectors should have a spare carrousel and a spare light bulb. There should be an extra extension cord handy. The speakers should have a pitcher of water and glasses at the lectern. And projection screens should be set into position if necessary.

Sales Person's Materials

On the day of he seminar, the sales people on duty should have all of their materials handy. They should have an ample supply of business cards in their pockets. They should also have the following items nearby:

- Quote forms
- Lead Cards
- Pens, pencils, and staplers
- Calculator
- Appointment book
- Presentation Notebooks
  1. *Product/Price Notebook*
  2. *Competition Book* (this should be used discreetly)
  3. *Answers to Frequently Asked Questions Notebook*
  4. *Publicity Notebook*
  5. *Customer Examples and References Notebook*
  6. *Extra Seminar Packets*

Rehearsal

The roles of each of the people involved in the seminar should be clearly delineated. If possible, a "walk through" rehearsal should be conducted to insure that everything is coordinated properly and that the props and equipment are in good working order. You'd be amazed at how many problems and mistakes can be avoided by this walk through. Remember, the more you "have your act together", the more the prospects will be impressed with you and your company.

Back up Systems

If you are using computers, slide projectors, or other automated equipment in your presentation, you should have a back-up plan if one or more of these pieces of equipment fail during your presentation. Unless you prepare for this eventuality, everyone involved in the presentation could be caught "off guard" with disastrous consequences. A well-prepared seminar has a complete back-up plan. Presenters coolly and calmly know exactly what to do in the event of a malfunction. Additionally, good marketers and sales people know how to turn such negative occurrences into positive advantages.

Follow up on RSVPs

Follow up is essential to successful attendance at the seminar. You will find that prospects who've RSVP'd that they will attend often need reminding or coaxing. Sales people should follow up at least once — one or two days before the seminar to re-confirm attendance. During the follow-up process, sales people can also "flush out" competitors posing as legitimate prospects. Every effort should be made to politely weed out competitors before the seminar because they can and will try to steal your prospects or disrupt your seminar if you let them.

The sales people should also use the follow-up opportunity to build a relationship with prospects and to find out what they want from the seminar.

SEMINAR PRESENTATION.

Dress for Success

In many cases, the first face-to-face contact prospects have with people from your company is at the seminar. This means that the appearance of all company personnel will make an all-important first impression on many of the attendees. Whatever your personal opinions about dress and grooming, they play a critical role in shaping prospects' opinions about your company. Professional looking suits for men and women are the rule when representing the company at a seminar or trade show. Dark suits are preferable to light ones (although lighter shades of gray are considered professional). White shirts or blouses are preferred, but other light colors, such as light blue or yellow are also acceptable. Dark ties are considered more professional, but light ones have climbed on the acceptability list in recent years (as long as they aren't "wild and crazy"). As a general rule, the clothes of company personnel should not stand out in a negative or unprofessional sort of way. While the guidelines for professional dress change over time, the above suggestions are timeless and safe.

Greeting and Screening

On the day of the seminar, a person should welcome attendees and make sure that they either sign a guest book with their name, position, company name and phone number and/or turn in a business card containing the same information. After the seminar, this information will be used by sales people to follow up. The marketing department will also use it to measure the success of the seminar.

Presentation

The presenter, or presenters, should be knowledgeable, confident, and skillful at speaking, but should not be too polished. Speakers that are too polished give a plastic, unreal, and "canned" appearance which raises questions about their sincerity. Presenters should command the interest and attention of the audience by being sharp, concise and clear in their presentation. They should be responsive to questions from the audience, but shouldn't allow any attendees to dominate the floor. Speakers must retain control at all times.

Sales Assistance

Before, during and after the seminar, sales personnel should be stationed at convenient places in the room to answer any questions that arise or to help the presenter with any props used in the presentation. You want to communicate to attendees that your company is populated by a team of competent and well-coordinated professionals.

At the end of the presentation, the presenter should encourage prospects to stay to ask any questions of the sales people and/or to enjoy the food and drink.

Clean Up

If the seminar is presented in the company's offices, arrangements should be made for clean up so that the facility is in presentable condition for the next day's work. Marketing good impressions doesn't end with the seminar.

FOLLOW UP.

After the seminar, follow up is critical. In fact, it is best for sales people to schedule the next step (which may be a phone call or face-to-face demonstration) with prospects even before they leave at the end of the seminar. To this end, sales people should have their appointment books and lead cards handy so they can record the next step to be taken. It's best to "strike while the iron is hot". Prospects cool off after they leave a seminar or demonstration and get colder as more time passes. Therefore, even if it is not possible to schedule the next step on the day of the seminar, sales people should call the next day to find out prospect reactions and schedule that next step.

Some companies do a good job of conducting seminars. Fewer do a good job of follow up. Without follow up, the efforts invested in the seminar will largely by wasted.

SEMINAR SUMMARY.

Seminars are one of the most effective ways of promoting high-tech products. More than media advertising, they enable companies to focus on specific market targets; they provide a good forum for educating and selling many prospects with a single coordinated presentation by the company's most effective speakers; and they serve as an excellent opportunity for company marketing and sales personnel to develop a personal relationship with target prospects. Furthermore, they are typically much less expensive than other forms of marketing.

WHAT ARE TRADE SHOWS?

Trade shows are exhibitions conducted in public places, such as major convention centers and hotels, whereby your company can exhibit its products along with other companies, many of whom are competitors. They are similar to seminars in the sense that they provide your company with a one-on-many sales opportunity. Unlike seminars, it draws a much larger audience, and your company must share the spotlight with many others. In the case of trade shows, however, the competition can be a positive element. That is, trade shows use the marketing principle of "cumulative attraction" to draw large numbers of prospects. More specifically, cumulative attraction is the principle by which many companies located close together will draw larger audiences than the same companies separated by some distance. Prospects are attracted by the opportunity to find out about the products of many different companies without spending the time and effort to travel between their offices. Moreover, prospects can conveniently comparison shop and make quicker buying decisions. Auto retailers understand this principle. That's why they often locate their showrooms in close proximity to each other.

Shows that target specific niches are particularly effective for companies whose products have been developed for the same niches.

OBJECTIVES.

There are many good reasons for a company to participate in a trade show. They include the following:

Sales

The ultimate marketing objective is to make more sales and satisfy more customers. While sales are made at trade shows, the longer lead times involved in selling certain products, typically preclude quick sales.

Leads

In the absence of closing sales at the show, the next best objective is to obtain "leads" which will hopefully turn into sales. Sales people working the show should have a stack of lead cards (see Figure 8-5) on which they can staple prospects' business cards. If the prospect does not furnish a business card, the sales person should make sure that they fill in the necessary information on the lead card, making sure to note the next step on the back.

If the show is very busy with heavy traffic, the sales person should have clever ways to avoid spending too much time with any one prospect. If the sales person senses that the prospect is very "hot" and insists on spending time asking questions, the sales person should spend the time. After all, "a bird in the hand is worth two in the bush."

The best strategy, however, is for the sales person to use the show to obtain leads, and to schedule appointments with those "hot" prospects at a more convenient time away from the hectic and distracting environment of the show.

Image

In addition to making sales and generating leads, an important objective of participation in a trade show is to spread the company name and improve its image. Companies who don't attend important trade shows miss opportunities to drive their name and position in the minds of attendees. If they are known, they are conspicuous by their absence. If they are not, they are less likely to become known.

Find Employees

Shows attract many of a company's publics in addition to prospects and customers. It is sometimes a good source of finding employees, vendors, and other groups of people who can help the company. Therefore, the sales people and others who have booth duty should be trained as to how to properly handle non-prospect inquiries. The most impressive and successful companies always give the impression they "have their act together". That is, they are always prepared.

THE SHOW PLAN.

To achieve these objectives, a show manager should be appointed from your marketing ranks to develop and execute a Show Plan. This plan should do the following:

1. Identify the trade shows which your company should attend.

2. Determine of the amount of space your company should occupy at each show.

3. Select key locations for each show.

4. Finalize the type and style of booth that you should bring to each show.

5. Prepare a schedule of critical steps required to participate in each show (including deadlines for completing show paperwork and mailing deposits to show sponsors).

6. Develop a checklist system for insuring that all booths, displays, equipment and show materials will be available and installed by the start of each show.

7. Develop a staffing plan for each show.

8. Instruct marketing and sales people on their show assignments and responsibilities.

9. Prepare a budget for all trade shows with subtotals for each individual show.

10. Develop a system for monitoring the success of each show.

11. Incorporate a mechanism for measuring the results of each show and determining if the company will participate in the same shows next time.

TRADE SHOW ESSENTIALS.

To achieve the objectives of the show plan the following marketing vehicles need to be developed:

Classy, Good-Looking Booth

The first thing prospects and other publics will notice about the company at a trade show is the booth. Therefore, careful attention should be given to the design of the booth. It should be both attractive and make people feel comfortable. If the company has a limited budget, a smaller high-quality booth is preferable to a big poor-quality booth. A classy good-looking booth can be made from low-cost, lightweight panels combined with live plants and trees.

As with all marketing instruments, the booth should be positioned to create the correct image of the company and to get the company's message into the minds of its various publics.

The booth should be designed to be functional (allow for product demonstrations), inviting (stand out from the crowd and attract attention), provide storage for show supplies and product spares (locked areas behind booth walls and in display cabinets), allow space for prospects to sit and talk with sales people (a show is a real foot killer), and provide sufficient space for effective foot traffic (however a crowded booth serves the company better than one that looks empty).

Booth panels can be created by incorporating company logos, blown-up photos from brochures and ads, and text from ads and brochures. No matter how it's constructed, the booth should tell the company's story in the best way possible. It should explain the company's history and track record as well as product benefits so that people who don't have the time to speak with your booth personnel can still learn about your company and products. This can be done via text screened on the walls of the booth or by the display of product and company literature.

Literature

All booths should have literature that can be handed to prospects. This literature should include your less-expensive product descriptions, price lists, and customer case histories. You should put your most expensive literature out of the reach of prospects. The reason is that many of them will walk by your booth and merely stuff these expensive brochures in their plastic and never look at them again. For those prospects who are seriously interested in your products, you can discreetly give them copies of your "best stuff" if they are willing to give you their business cards (or fill out your lead cards) so that you can follow up on their interest.

Promotions

Many companies offer promotions as an incentive for attendees to order product at the show. The marketing pieces created for these promotions follow the same processes as the development of print ads and other product literature.

MEASURING RESULTS.

As with all marketing, the success of each trade show should be measured so that a decision can be intelligently made as to whether to participate in the next show by the same show sponsors. Leads, demonstrations or appointments, and sales resulting from show contacts should be measured and reported from the sales staff to the senior marketing (or trade show) executive.

SUGGESTED EXERCISES.
1. Collect several invitations to company seminars.
2. Do the same for information packets.
3. Of the invitations and packets you collect, rank them according to which are the most effective.
4. Write down the reasons for your ranking.
5. Create an invitation for a seminar given by your organization.
6. Put together an information packet for this seminar.

Chapter 12 • PUBLICITY

"The best advertising is free advertising..."

Good publicity is even more effective than good advertising. It has the air of objectivity. It is often better remembered, and it prompts quicker buying actions.

Whenever possible, it should be quoted in company advertising. This will multiply the positive effect of the publicity and create even greater buyer awareness.

As with word-of-mouth referrals, publicity should be pursued actively. What steps should the marketing department take to foster positive publicity? The following is a sample list:

IDENTIFY MEDIA.

The first step is to do some marketing research to find out the publications which your target markets read. Again, this market research does not have to cost a lot of money. Asking your customers and prospects which publications they read will usually do the job. You should record their answers on a piece of paper and tally up the numbers for each publication mentioned. Those that were mentioned most frequently should be targeted for all your publicity releases. Once you've identified the primary media which influence your market targets, you should enter key information on these publications into your mailing list data base. The essential information in this data base should include the following: the type of media, the name of the publication or broadcast network, the editor's name, the technical editor's name (if your product is a technical one) mailing address, and phone number(s). Additional useful information might include the number of market targets in the publication's audience, general circulation figures, the editor's birthday, special comments about the media, and publication dates of publicity on your company.

ESTABLISH MEDIA CONTACTS.

You should make an effort to meet with and get to know the editor, writers, and other key personnel who work for each of the media identified above. These media people should be considered one of your publics and should be invited to company functions and parties, receive company newsletters, and receive all company general-purpose mailings. If the publication prints or broadcasts positive stories about your company or publishes articles written by company personnel, you should send the editor and the writer(s) a thank you note. As with your other publics, the idea is to build personal relationships with people in the media.

PRESS RELEASES.

Press releases about company products and achievements should be sent to the media list on a regular basis. If available and applicable, an 8 x 10 glossy photo of the product or subject should accompany each press release.

Guidelines for Creating Effective Press Releases

For press releases to be effective, they should follow certain established guidelines. Press releases should be:

- **Factual and avoid puffery**. Exaggerations and other forms of puffery should not be included in news releases. Publications will often refuse to print product claims which appear to be overstated. They receive many "stories" and are skeptical of and sensitive to anything that hints of bias or exaggeration.

- **Newsworthy**. Old news (a contradiction in and of itself) is not likely to be printed. Therefore, it's important for the information in your release to be sent to the media on a timely basis.

- **Brief**. As per the UMS, news releases which are clear and concise are more likely to be printed than "padded" ones which are too lengthy. It's not the number of words or pages which determine the brevity of a release; it's the economy of words used to cover the subject matter. Many concise releases are several pages long because they cover a complex and extensive subject. Other "wordy" releases are contained within one page.

- **Quotable.** Most releases contain identified quotes from authoritative executives in the company. For example, "According to John Smith, XYZ Corp's Director of Marketing, 'This new product represents a real breakthrough in the manufacture of super-conductive materials.'" or "Mary Jones, ABC Corp's CEO, claims, 'This new low-calorie butter substitute will satisfy a multi-billion dollar world-wide demand.'"

- **Memorable.** Unless the release grabs the editor's attention, it will not be published. As with all marketing pieces, headlines with hooks should be included in press releases. Unlike marketing to your target audience, however, the target of your Press Release is the editor of the publication or program. You want to sell editors on including your news in their publication.

In addition to following these guidelines, press releases should utilize a long-established format. This format is described below.

Press Release Format

A well-structured press release follows a standard format. This format typically includes the following:

- **Pre-printed News Sheets.** Press releases appear more professional if the company (or it's publicity firm) has pre-printed news-sheets with the name of the company followed by the word "NEWS" at the top of these sheets. Many companies use the same sheets for news releases that they employ for the cover page of their news letters.

- **Heading Identifier.** Under the pre-printed "COMPANY NAME/NEWS", should be a heading identifier which contains the company name, address, phone, and name and position of the contact person, which is usually the Director of Marketing or public relations representative.

- **Timing of the Release.** After the heading identifier, the timing of the release is indicated (usually on the left side of the page). Probably the most frequently-used timing indicator is "For Immediate Release" since most releases are designed to generate news coverage as soon as possible. In some cases, however, especially when a company wants to "leak" a story to the press, it will highlight a restrictive timing such as Not to be released for publication for 60 days from the date of this release. In addition to leaking the story, the company may issue a restrictive timing to insure that the publication will have sufficient time and leave adequate space for including this news.

- **Headline.** After the timing of the release and skipping two or three lines, the actual press release officially begins with its headline. As stated above, the headline follows the guidelines and concepts of the UMS. A sample headline might read, "ICM Introduces the 'Electronic Secretary'."

- **Body Text.** Skipping two or three lines after the headline, the body text of the release begins. All body text should be double-spaced. The reason for this is so the editor can easily make corrections.

- **Location, Date, and Company Identifiers.** The first two lines of the body text begin with identification of the location, date, and company identifiers. For example, "Armonk, New York, December 1, 2001. International Computer Machines Corporation (ICM), a manufacturer of small and large computer systems for business, announced the introduction of its long-awaited 'Electronic Secretary'."

- **Page Numbers.** All pages of the release should be numbered for quick reference.

- **Shelf-life Identifier.** At the bottom of the last page of the release should be a "shelf-life" identifier which tells the editor of the publication how long the news is expected to be newsworthy. This is very important for magazines whose material deadlines can be up to 60 days prior to publication. If the news will be newsworthy for a long or indefinite period of time a "- ## -" identifier is put on the bottom center of the last page of the release. If the news will be news for 30 days after publication a "-30-" identifier is used, and so forth.

- **Product Protection.** With the introduction of new products, it is very important that the product name have the proper protection identifier as a raised superscript to the right of the first use of the name in the release. For a trademarked name, an "R" in a circle should be used if the trademark is officially registered. Until registration is official, a "TM" is used to indicate that the name is a trademark of the company. An example of a product name with this latter trademark identifier is shown below:

ELECTRIC BRIEFCASE™.

The "™" will protect the name, and if someone violates your trademark rights, you can collect "full damages" if you win the litigation. The primary advantage of a registered trademark (®) is that you can collect triple damages should you win a trademark violation case.

As you probably already know, in addition to protecting the name, you should protect your product with applicable patents before publicizing the product's existence. You should confer with a reputable patent attorney for more details about obtaining patents and trademarks. Get more than one opinion and more than one price quote when shopping for such an attorney.

An example of a Press Release which uses many of the above format elements and guidelines is shown in *Figure 12-1*.

Once created, the Press Release should be sent to the appropriate media on your mailing list. In most cases, they are all appropriate since it does not cost much to send your release to them all.

PRESS RELEASE

ENCORE VIDEO INDUSTRIES **NEWS**

July 15, 1987

Contact: Ira Kalb
          Encore Video Industries
          6344 Fountain Avenue
          Hollywood, CA 90028

<u>For Immediate Release</u>

ENCORE VIDEO INDUSTRIES INTRODUCES EPR SYSTEM

Encore Video Industries, Inc., Hollywood, CA, a manufacturer and marketer of telecine products, announced the formal introduction of its EPR™ (Electronic Pin Registration) system.

According to EVI's Executive Vice President, Ira Kalb, "the EPR system enables you to do pin-registered film to video tape transfers in real time! Unlike other registration alternatives on the market, EPR does not encumber the telecine in any way. You turn it on with the flick of a switch, and you turn it off the same way. When it's off, the telecine operates as before. When it's on, it perfectly registers the film at the telecine's real time speed of from 16 to 30 frames per second. EPR enables you to do composites in a fraction of the time of other registration methods. What's more, it enables you to take on projects you have not been able to do because of a slow and cumbersome, or non-existent, registration system."

The system is a software-based system that can be upgraded with new features and improvements over time.

EVI's parent company, Encore Video, has been using the prototype of this system with considerable success in its post production business over the past year and one-half.

The basic EPR system sells for $100,000. Options include: (1) an FVS 100 (Film to Video Sequencer) for $10,000 which guarantees proper sequencing of "3:2 Pull down" when the film is transferred to video tape; and (2) a software maintenance agreement which covers all software updates for an annual fee of $2,500.

\#\#

Figure 12-1

ARTICLES.

Creating and sending press releases to your media list is one way to obtain free publicity for your company. Having articles published about your company and products is another.

Articles about your products and company fall into two general categories — (1) those written by publication writers and (2) those written by personnel from your company. The difference between the two is that you typically have more control over the information in the latter case (that is, if the editor does not decide to make too many changes to your articles).

Unsophisticated marketers wait for articles to be written about their products and company. Savvy marketers don't. What do they do to get articles written? The following steps are typically employed:

Issue Press Releases

Press Releases can interest media in doing an entire article about your company and product(s).

Make Personal Contacts

Developing and maintaining personal contacts with key media personnel, such as editors and certain writers, will help to position your company and products in their minds when they write articles.

Hire Free-lance Writers

Free-lance writers whose articles frequently appear in target publications can be hired to write articles for the company. From their prior work, they have close contacts with key people in the media. As a result of these contacts, they can often get the articles placed more easily and quickly than you can.

Encourage Company Writers

Good writers in the company should be identified and encouraged to write articles about the company and its products. The marketing department should get these articles placed in the magazines on the media list. The steps involved in doing this include the following:

- **Obtain Editorial Calendars from all targeted media.** As shown in *Figure 12-2*, Editorial Calendars list the editorial focus of all upcoming issues by date.

- **Distribute Calendars to Writers.** Once these calendars are received copies can be distributed to the "writers" in the company.

- **Encourage Writers.** Many people write articles to express their points of view, see their names in print, promote themselves, and for a variety of other reasons. Whatever the reasons, the company should offer writers a small bonus for all articles which are written and successfully placed in targeted media. This recognition, however small, is recognition nonetheless. It typically serves to encourage writers to help the company with its publicity efforts. It also serves to boost the self-esteem of writers and to make them feel closer to the company.

- **Select Topics on Which to Write.** These writers can select the topics and issues for which they would like to write articles.

- **Provide Schedules.** Marketing can provide them with the writing schedule and deadlines. If more than one writer would like to write on a particular subject matter, the additional writers should be encouraged. Their resultant articles can either be submitted for the same issue, or can be sent to other publications.

- **Include Biographies and Photos whenever possible.** Marketing should arrange to have flattering photos and bios prepared for each writer so they can accompany each article. Bios and photos increase the exposure of both the company and the writer and serve to make the articles more interesting to the target audience.

EDITORIAL CALENDER

```
                    1989 EDITORIAL CALENDAR


JANUARY    :  Posting Episodic Television    Space     : Dec   1
           ·  Pre-AFM/Location Expo Report   Materials : Dec   8

FEBRUARY   :  Producers' Guide: Camera RentalSpace     : Jan   2
              Bonus Dist: Location Expo       Materials : Jan   9

MARCH      :  Television Producers Spotlite   Space     : Feb   1
              Bonus Disc: NAB                 Materials : Feb   8

APRIL      :  Producers' Guide: Telecine      Space     : Mar   1
                                              Materials : Mar   8

MAY        :  Special Effects Producers       Space     : Apr   3
              Spotlite; Audio Sweatening      Materials : Apr  10

JUNE       :  Producers' Guide: Lighting      Space     : May   1
              NAB Product Review              Materials : May   8
              Bonus Dist: ShowBiz Expo

JULY       :  Commercial Producers Spotlite   Space     : June  1
                                              Materials : June  8

AUGUST     :  Producers' Guide: Future        Space     : July  3
              of Post                         Materials : Jul  10

SEPTEMBER  :  Motion Picture Producers        Space     : Aug   1
              Spotlite                        Materials : Aug   8

OCTOBER    :  Producers' Guide: Editing;      Space     : Sept  1
              Latest in Grip                  Materials : Sept  8
              Bonus Dist: SMPTE Convention .

NOVEMBER   :  Music Video Producers Spotlite  Space     : Oct   2
              Bonus Dist: American Video      Materials : Oct   9
                          Conference

DECEMBER   :  Producers' Guide: Lighting      Space     : Nov   1
              & Grip Equipment                Materials : Nov   8
```

Figure 12-2

BROADCAST MEDIA.

Particularly worthy news items should be released to TV and Radio broadcast media via your Press Release. Products that are new, unusual, visually appealing, or revolutionary are good candidates for attracting interest from the broadcast media.

PUBLIC DISPLAY.

All positive publicity on the company and its employees should be publicly displayed in the lobby and in the halls of company offices. The best articles should be permanently framed and displayed in areas, such as the main lobby, which are frequently visited by prospects and customers. This publicity serves to help sell your company and products by letting your publics know that your products and company have been recognized by established media.

Publicity should also be displayed in attractive "Publicity Notebooks" located in the lobby and other public gathering places. While prospects are in the lobby waiting to speak with a sales or support person, they often "browse through" the Publicity Notebooks. The positive publicity which they see helps to sell them on the company's products. Reprints of particularly favorable articles should be made for dissemination to prospects and customers.

SALES AIDS.

Publicity Notebooks should also be made available to sales personnel for use in their sales presentations. They are invaluable in helping to support product and company benefit statements made by sales people. They provide "independent" validation and credibility to what the sales people tell their prospects.

An ample supply of reprints of favorable publicity should be kept in central sales files. When appropriate, these should be sent to prospects with personally-typed letters to answer objections and to help close sales.

TRAINING.

Positive publicity should be included in the training materials used to train new personnel. Many companies overlook the fact that employees are a very important public of the company. Just as other publics, they need to be "sold" on the company and its products. They would like to believe that they made the correct job choice and that they work for an excellent company. Positive publicity will help to convince and reassure them.

MATERIAL FOR ADS.

Sometimes writers of articles and news pieces on your products come up with excellent headlines, hooks, or slogans which you can use in your ads and brochures. In fact, quoting them in your ad is even more effective because its "they say" rather than "you say" advertising. That is, when "they say" it, the message has more credibility than when "you say" it.

NEWSLETTERS.

To increase the exposure of your publics to your favorable publicity, you can reprint or refer to this publicity in your newsletters. In this way, you can improve the probability that your customers and other important publics are aware of your recognition.

COUNTERACT NEGATIVES.

No matter how good the company or its products, it will receive negative publicity at some time or another. If it is undeserved, it is up to marketing to insure that these negatives be counteracted quickly with retractions and positive publicity. If it is deserved, the company should not bury the problem. It should look for ways to turn the negatives into positives. This is typically accomplished by admitting the problem, apologizing, developing a plan to correct the problem, correcting the problem in a positive way (usually by giving the public something more than they had before), and informing the public of your positive actions.

A good example of a company who effectively turned negative publicity into a public relations "coup," is *Johnson & Johnson's* handling of the *Tylenol scare*. Some years ago, a maniac was filling *Tylenol* capsules with poison. As a result, many people got very ill, and several people died. Rather than deny the problem, the CEO of the company went on television to admit the problem, apologize to the public, order that all applicable products be removed from store shelves, and unveil a plan to permanently solve the tampering problem with tamper-proof packaging. While these actions hurt sales in the short run, they served to restore confidence in the product and greatly enhance the company's image in the eyes of the public. Rather than "kill" the product, the company looked at the negative situation as an opportunity to turn it into a much larger positive. The strategy has paid off with the company recording long-term product sales and profits that have far surpassed pre-incident levels.

SUMMARY.

One of the best attributes of Publicity is it is "free". More importantly, it is has proven to be more effective than advertising and other forms of Promotion because it has more credibility. Therefore, your company should have a well-coordinated plan to generate as much positive publicity as possible. This plan should include sending press releases at regular intervals to targeted media; encouraging company personnel, independent writers, and publication staff writers to routinely write and publish articles on the company and it's products; displaying and distributing examples of positive publicity to the company's various publics; and counteracting any negative publicity by "turning negatives into positives".

SELECTED EXERCISES

1. Identify target publications which your key publics often read. Call a few prospects and customers to get the names of these publications.

2. Find the names of the editors, the addresses, and phone numbers of these publications. Enter them on your mailing list data base.

3. Contact these publications and ask them to send you a copy of their Editorial Calendars. Also ask them if they will send you copies of two or three non-confidential press releases for this assignment.

4. Compose a press release on a newsworthy product or subject according to the format discussed above or the format from one of the press releases you have collected.

5. Select an article that attracted your attention from one of your target publications. List the reasons why you believe it is a good article.

Notes.

Chapter 13 • DIRECT MAIL

"It can be less expensive, and you know where it's going..."

WHAT IS DIRECT MAIL?

Direct mail is a form of advertising whereby a marketing piece (such as a letter, brochure, catalogue, special "mailer" and/or product sample) is sent directly to targeted prospects.

ADVANTAGES.

Direct mail affords you certain advantages over media advertising and some other forms of marketing. It enables you to:

Focus on specific market targets

Whereas media advertising is a "broad-brush" method which covers an entire audience or geographic segment, direct mail is a "rifle shot" approach which allows you to focus on specific names and addresses that have been identified as targets.

You can compile or purchase mailing lists from a variety of sources which enable you to target a specific industry, SIC (Standard Industry Classification) Code, Zip Code, or market segments with other similar characteristics.

Spend money on an incremental basis

With media advertising, you typically pay a lot of money to cover a media's entire audience. Although some media allow you to cover specific geographic territories, you still can't reach targets on an incremental basis. With Direct mail you can. To reach one more prospect, you merely pay for the cost of one more mailer plus the postage to mail it. In this way, if you don't have the budget to send your mailing piece to a large segment of your targeted list, you can still effectively reach some additional prospects.

Increase comprehension of at least part of your message

Since target prospects have to make a conscious decision to read, file or throw away your mailing piece, they are more likely to see or absorb something about your message than they would if they were thumbing through magazines, driving past billboards, or switching radio and TV channels. Even if they decide to throw it away, in making their decision, they will usually see your company and product name. If the piece is well-done, your company and product name is likely to enter their minds in a positive context. Over repeated mailings, the cumulative impact can be very positive and lead to subsequent buying actions.

Maintain control over the list (data base)

With the proper system, you can create and maintain your own mailing list. You can add, change or delete names to your list at will. You can sort your list according to specific criteria, such as product interest and zip code, and use it to send mailings to specific target segments. You can re-use the entries whenever you wish. However, if you rent or license use of list from a mailing list company, you may be required to pay additional fees to re-use the list. You can legally avoid these fees if you are clever in creating your mailing piece. That is, if you are successful in getting prospects to respond to your mailing, they become your prospects. Therefore, by offering a strong incentive for responding (such as a free gift or discount on purchase of the product), you can add them to your own list and avoid paying additional fees for further use of these entries.

Enclose product literature

Unlike media advertising which often requires a new ad slick or velox to be developed for each publication's format, direct mail enables you to send existing product brochures and technical literature to prospective buyers with a carefully focused cover letter.

Use it in conjunction with other marketing pieces

In addition to using direct mail for its own marketing purposes, it is also an effective means of distributing other marketing pieces. Direct mail techniques are frequently used for sending seminar invitations to target prospects, newsletters to various publics, press releases to target media, and product literature and samples to prospective buyers.

Begin a Relationship

Sending letters to targets is an excellent way to begin a marketing or business relationship. Unlike the interruptive nature of "cold calling" on the telephone, mailers enable you to introduce yourself, your products and company, in a non-interruptive way. That is, a letter or mailing piece can be opened and read by the prospect when and if he/she chooses. A letter can be re-read for better understanding, and can be saved for future reference. The product literature which accompanies a cover letter can have pictures of the product which, if properly composed, "are worth thousands of words" of print or dialogue.

Perform market tests

Since the prospects who receive mailings can be carefully selected, direct mail is a good vehicle for conducting product and market tests. Since broad-brush marketing approaches cannot be as selective, they are not as good as direct mail for conducting such tests.

POTENTIAL PROBLEMS.

With the above advantages, there are several problems that can arise from use of direct mail. Examples include the following:

You don't know what happens to it after it arrives

While you know where it was sent, you don't know what happens to it after it arrives at its destination. The targeted prospect may have moved; a protective secretary may label your piece as "junk mail" and bury it in a pile of other junk mail or throw it away; or a colleague may intercept it and file it away somewhere or toss it in the trash.

It takes considerable effort to properly maintain a mailing list.

Getting all names, titles, genders and addresses correct is a very big chore. It not only requires correct entry of original data; it also involves making timely changes as they occur. People move around, change names, and positions. Companies also change names and locations.

If not properly entered and maintained, incorrect mailing data can be quite costly — not only in wasted postage, but also in damaging public relations. Instead of developing positive relationships with prospects, mailings which misspell names, misidentify genders and positions, and/or send duplicate mailings to the same person can have the opposite effect. While it may cost a little more to properly enter and maintain mailing data, the cost is small in comparison the damage that incorrect mailing data can cause.

It's not easy to distinguish your mailing from "junk mail".

Prospects receive so much mail from unsolicited sources, many have a tendency to throw this mail in the trash without properly evaluating it. The challenge to every marketer, therefore, is to create a mailing piece or package which will be given a proper evaluation.

The remainder of this Chapter will present techniques and suggestions for creating successful mailing pieces — that is, mailing pieces which survive the dreaded "circular file" to make a positive impact on targeted prospects.

CREATING THE SUCCESSFUL MAILING PIECE.

While a mailing piece can be anything from a personally-typed letter to a slick self-mailer, the formula for success is basically the same. It should be developed in accordance with the marketing plan, general marketing principles, and the UMS. In light of these guidelines, the more important variables to be decided upon when developing the mailer include:

- **Numbers.** How many are to be produced? This will depend on the numbers in your target audience, the size of the mailing lists selected, the number of times the mailing will be repeated, the quantity price breaks to produce the mailing piece, and your budget.

- **Repeats.** How many repeat mailings should be sent? This depends on so many different factors that there is no "hard and fast" rule. Some experts believe that for a mailing to be effective, it has to be sent to a prospect an average of seven times over some period of time. While the number of repeat mailings can be debated, most mailing experts agree that responses can be boosted significantly by some number of repeats to the same prospect. For example, a seminar invitation should be sent out only once with follow up phone calls to increase response. A newsletter should be sent out once per issue according to its normal frequency (usually monthly or quarterly). On the other hand, a self-mailer may require two or three repeats in order to achieve the desired results.

- **Intervals.** At what intervals should repeat mailings be sent? Again, this will vary depending on the specific circumstances. If the mailing contains an offer that will expire, the expiration date will help you to determine the necessary intervals. If the mailer being sent is to create market awareness and sales over the longer run, the mailings might be spread out over longer intervals.

- **Response Card.** Will a response card or coupon be attached or enclosed? There should always be some sort of response mechanism. The best results are achieved if the mailing address, phone number (preferably 800-number), and return coupon are all provided. To later measure the effectiveness of the mailing, a special pre-printed code should be included on the response card to indicate the specific mailing from which it originated.

- **Pre-paid Return Postage.** Will return postage be prepaid by the company, or will the prospect have to affix postage? Pre-paid postage will generate a better response. While the bulk rate for thousands of returned response cards can add up to a significant amount of money, it's a small price to pay for a prospect who can be converted into a sale or a fan of the company. Relative to the time and money spent on the mailing, it's not so significant. Therefore, why risk losing a prospect at the last crucial step? It's a good idea for the company to pay for the return postage.

- **Size.** Will it be the standard envelope size? Post card size? Invitation size? Brochure size? Some other size? The answer depends on the information to be included, the product being advertised, the costs of the various alternatives, and the positioning strategy.

- **Envelope.** Will it be placed in an envelope (known as a *solo* mailing) or will an address label be put directly onto the mailer (known as a *self-mailer*)? This depends on so many different factors. An envelope avoids worrying about having the mailing label interfere with the information on the mailer. It also helps to distinguish the piece from "junk mail". On the other hand, it makes integration of the coded address label with the return coupon more difficult. It also involves an additional operation — stuffing the envelopes. All other things being equal, the envelope will usually improve the response.

- **Quality.** High, medium or low? Remember image and position. If less than high-quality is selected, a good reason should be given in the piece — i.e. "To hold costs down and pass the savings on to you...", "To avoid costly delays in sending this important information to you...", "To help conserve environmental resources...", etc.

- **Reward.** Will a reward be offered for returning? For example, a free booklet, coffee mug, pen, etc. As long as the reward is useful, nominal and free, it will boost response. This is particularly important if you are renting the mailing list and you need to be able to legally put as many prospects as possible on your own list.

- **Color.** Will the mailer be in color or black and white? If in color, will it be two-color or four color? While many believe that color works better than black & white, others prefer black & white. With high-tech and many other products, black, white, and various shades of gray (which are the same to the printer as black & white) can be very effective. It is certainly safer than selecting the "wrong" color or using cheap-looking colors. And it is much less expensive. Generally, a high-quality black & white piece is much more effective than a low or mediocre-quality color piece. A very popular and effective technique is to use black and white (and shades of gray) with a single color added as an accent (this color is often the color of the product).

- **Pages.** How many pages or panels will it have? This depends on the amount of text, pictures and the desired space. Fewer words and more space is the most effective.

- **Folds.** How will the mailer be folded? While this may seem as if it's a trivial issue, it's not. It depends on the number of pages, or panels, in the mailer, whether or not there is a response card attached, the most convenient way to print, and what information is to be on the front and back covers. A four-panel mailer is folded once usually down the middle. A six-panel mailer is folded twice. The most common method is to fold the right most panel inward. However, some six-panel mailers are folded like an accordion, whereby the right-most panel is folded back.

- **Words.** How many words and how much space? Brevity and simplicity are most effective. The sharper the message the quicker it will penetrate the minds of prospects.

- **Pictures.** Will it contain pictures or just have words? If the product is good looking and professional models are used in the pictures, the "pictures are worth thousands of words". If not, pictures will only deter from the message. If the subjects of the pictures are not particularly good-looking they can be photographed through special lenses and filters. After the photo is taken, they can be reproduced with special patterned screens to make them look more appealing. Another alternative is to substitute an illustration for a photo of the subject.

MAILING PIECE EXAMPLE.

Figures 13-1 and 13-2 show a direct mailing piece that was created for Compal, Inc. by its ad agency, Haller/Schwarz. The mailer was created for the legal market, one of Compal's target markets. Designed like a brochure, this mailer differs only in the size and format of the piece. That is, it is designed to be folded into six sides that will fit into a standard business-sized envelope.

Cover

Headline: The cover, right-most or top panel in *Figure 13-1,* has a headline which clearly focuses on a specific target market — law firms. It uses legal-oriented language as a hook (although it's not a particularly strong hook).

Company Logo: The standard company logo is the only other element on the cover. While the background of the cover is in a high-tech light gray, the logo background has been reversed to emphasize the 45-degree angle and to help "stamp" this logo in the minds of prospects.

Inside

Body Text: The body text of the mailer is contained in *Figure 13-2.* At the time the mailer was created in the late 1970's, the small business marketplace was still a little nervous about computers. This mailer is sensitive to that situation. It speaks to lawyers about the benefits of the computer in their own language — not in computer language which they may not understand. It makes an aggressive offer in the second inside panel. It allows customers to return the system within a month for almost a full refund (less one month's lease plus delivery and training costs) if they are dissatisfied. This offer is a good and serious one. It's better than a free trial for a number of reasons. A free trial attracts prospects who are not always seriously

MAILER FRONT & BACK

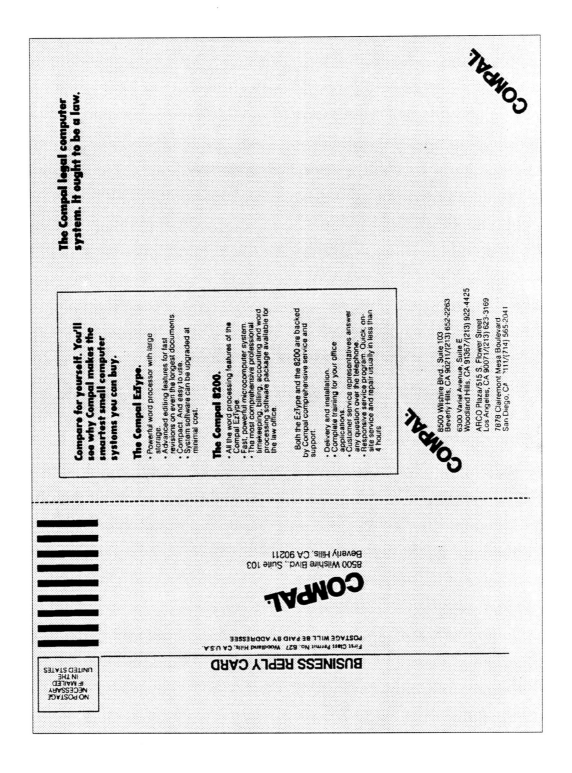

Figure 13-1

MAILER INSIDE

I think it's criminal for an attorney to be without a Compal legal computer system.
Tell me more about The Compal Difference.

NAME
NAME OF FIRM
ADDRESS
CITY
STATE   ZIP
TELEPHONE NO.

No attorney today should have to work without a Compal legal computer system. Contracts. Interrogatories. Depositions. Correspondence. A Compal computer system can save you time, trouble and effort. Choose the Compal EzType™ for word processing. Or the Compal 8200 for word processing, timekeeping and billing.

The fact is, there's no better way to help a hardworking law office handle all the work.

Compal. We know legal computer systems like you know the law.

Compal is the recognized leader in complete small computer systems.

No one knows better than Compal what attorneys really need. And no other small computer system can offer you better performance. And features.

Both the Compal EzType word processor and the Compal 8200 microcomputer have been thoroughly tested. And proven in hundreds of law offices.

So when you buy a Compal, you never buy a system that was introduced just yesterday. Or will be obsolete tomorrow.

What's more, Compal systems are designed to enhance even the finest office environment. Which means that a Compal not only works smart. It helps you look smart, too.

Put us on trial. And judge for yourself.

We're so confident that a Compal system will work for you, we're willing to guarantee it. Buy one, and use it for a month. If your Compal system hasn't helped you handle your workload faster, we'll refund the purchase price. You only pay for delivery, training and your first month's lease.

No other computer company can make that kind of an offer. Because no other computer company can sell you a Compal computer system.

The Compal Difference. There's only one place to find it.

Hardware. Software. Training. And service. That's The Compal Difference. To find out more, send the enclosed card today.

Figure 13-2

interested. It also places all the risk and all the cost on the shoulders of the company. Moreover, with a free trial, many prospects are skeptical about the quality of the product since they assume that the company is acting "too hungry" in its efforts to sell it.

Close: After being interested by the trial offer in the previous section, the close of the mailer solicits action by asking the reader to send in the "enclosed card today" for more information.

Format: The inside body text is cleanly laid out and concise. Boldface sub-headlines emphasize the most important points. There is sufficient white space, and the photo and text integrate quite well. Since this photo has been discussed in a previous section it is not repeated here.

Response Card

On the front side of the response card (Figure 13-1 at bottom), there are several important elements including the following:

Identification: To identify to the prospect and the postal authorities that this is a response card, the words **"BUSINESS REPLY CARD"** are printed on the front of this card.

Postage Permit: Just below the identification of the card is the mailing permit and postage information.

Company Name and Address: The company's name (in the form of its logo) and address are preprinted on the card for the prospect's convenience. The choice of the logo on an angle instead of the simple company name is made to get the prospect to better remember the company name.

No postage necessary notice: A "no postage" notice is placed where the stamp would go to remind the prospect that they do not have to affix postage.

Since postage regulations often change, you should check with the post office to obtain a copy of the latest BUSINESS REPLY CARD requirements.

Back Cover

The back cover of the mailer is shown in the center panel of

Figure 13-1. Whether or not the response card is torn off and sent in, this panel will be the back cover once the mailer is folded. The cover contains the following elements:

Summary Product Information: Summary information on the products and services for lawyers.

Distribution: A list of company locations, with addresses and phone numbers which prospects can use to call or stop in for a demonstration.

Logo: The company logo. Please note that this logo probably would be better placed in the lower right corner. Perhaps it was moved to this location so it wouldn't interfere with the gray screen of the front cover when printed.

Envelope

To boost response of this mailing and to avoid having the mailing label interfere with the "look" of the mailer, the ad agency decided to put the mailer in an envelope. As shown in *Figure 13-3*, the envelope has a phrase (that ties in with the headline of the mailer and focuses on the target market) at the bottom left corner of the envelope. This was designed as a *teaser* to interest prospects in opening the envelope and reading its contents. An inside address is also provided which lets prospects know something about the sender and the contents. It's important to give prospects an idea of what's inside since many resent being "tricked" into opening mail in which they have no interest.

Overall

Color: To reinforce the high-tech nature of the product and to hold down printing costs, the brochure was done in black and white (including shades of gray). It was felt that the image of the company and its products would be better served by putting money into quality paper stock, more expensive typesetting, a top photographer, and a larger mailing list rather than color printing.

Paper: The paper used was top-quality, brochure card stock with a semi-gloss finish which allows prospects to write on it. Quality paper holds the ink better, makes for better folds, and looks better after handling.

MAILER ENVELOPE

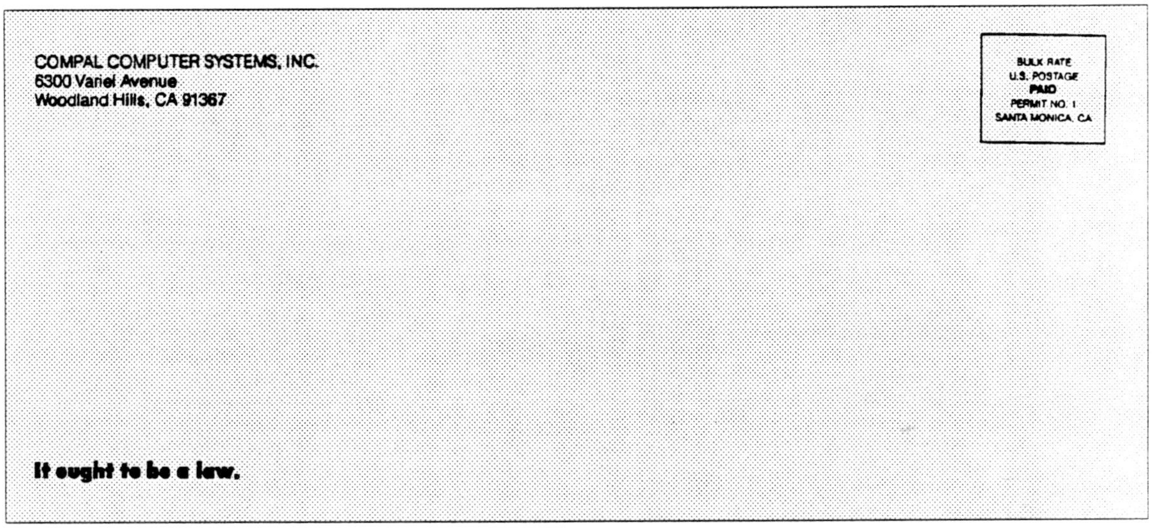

COMPAL COMPUTER SYSTEMS, INC.
6300 Variel Avenue
Woodland Hills, CA 91367

BULK RATE
U.S. POSTAGE
PAID
PERMIT NO. 1
SANTA MONICA, CA

It ought to be a law.

Figure 13-3

Photos: The photos used in the mailer were taken by a top photographer in his studio. To save money on photography costs (the photographer, the model, the ad agency art director, etc.), the same photo was used for a variety of different marketing pieces. In addition to holding down photography costs, the re-use of the same photo for different purposes reinforces identification of the product and company. For the same reason, companies often run ads with the same models or actors over and over again.

THE MAILING LIST.

In addition to having a good mailing piece, the quality of the mailing list is essential to a successful mailing. The quality of the mailing list is determined by a variety of factors including:

- *Coverage:* How well it covers the target market segments. Often times, it is difficult to exactly know what groups of people fit within your target market segments. It may take some experimentation with different lists to find out.

- *Accuracy:* How accurate are the names and addresses? People move, change positions and jobs. A mailing list is accurate if it is constantly maintained — i.e. as mailers are returned, the incorrect names and addresses should be corrected. Also many lists have genders and titles incorrectly stated. Almost nothing drives a person crazier than having their name misspelled or their gender or position incorrectly stated. Remember, the purpose of the mailer is to attract rather than alienate buyers so care should be taken to properly maintain and select mailing lists.

SELECTING THE MAILING LIST.

If you don't have an adequately large home-grown list, you are going to want to buy or rent mailing lists from mailing houses or list brokers. The advantage of using list brokers is that it is in their interest to find you the best lists to match your needs. If they don't, they know that they'll lose you as a customer.

If you want to do it yourself, there are many mailing list directories and catalogs which you can use to obtain information about specialized mailing lists. For example, CMG Information Services publishes a catalog of mailing lists for marketing to college professors, administrators and librarians. The reference librarian in any public library is a good place to start if you don't have another source for these mailing list catalogs. Better sources are the publications that your target markets read. They typically have quality prospects on their subscription lists.

Before making your final mailing list selection, you should make sure that the characteristics of the people on the list match the profiles of those in your target markets. Ideally, you would like to have breakdowns according: age, sex, income level, occupation, product interest, buying habits, and other factors relevant to your particular product. The lists which most closely match your target market profiles are the ones you should use. If more than one list matches your profiles equally well, you can make your decision based on the cost to reach every thousand prospects. Most mailing list companies charge on a cost per thousand basis.

MAILING HOUSES.

There are companies which provide a variety of mailing services including: picking up mailing pieces from the printer, folding, stapling, envelope stuffing, affixing postage, coding, selling or renting lists, maintaining lists, and eliminating duplicates from different lists. A simple cost effective analysis should be done to determine which, if any, mailing services are best accomplished inside and outside the company. For purposes of control, it is probably best to keep control over the mailing list itself inside the company.

BOOSTING RESPONSE.

A one percent response to a mailing is considered average. That is, if you send out 100 pieces, you are likely to get 1 response. In addition to the suggestions presented above with regard to the *design of the mailing piece* and the *selection of mailing lists* (doing a better job of targeting), response can be boosted significantly by the following:

- **Repeat mailings:** Even if a response is not forthcoming, the company and product names will get into the minds of prospects and make future sales easier. Different studies quote different statistics on repeat mailings so they won't be quoted here. They all agree, however, that repeat mailings boost response significantly — due to the cumulative nature of advertising.

- **Inbound Telemarketing (800-number):** On average, including an easily-visible 800-number in the mailing piece will boost response 50 percent.

- **Outbound Telemarketing (Phone follow-up):** The personal touch will always boost response. Each of the sales people, or telemarketing people (if the company has them), should be given equal sections of the lists in their territories to call.

- **Personal letter follow-up (if feasible):** With word processors, personal letters to large numbers of people are feasible. Sales people could send such letters to people in their sections of the list. Personal letters are an excellent way to follow up because they are non-interruptive and they give the prospects a chance to review them when time is available.

- **Personalized Gifts:** A technique which has been particularly effective for boosting mailing response is the enclosure of personalized gifts with each mailing package. The personalized gift may or may not tie-in with your company's products. It usually has the initials or nickname of the top executive to whom it is directed carved or engraved on it. Because the mailer comes in a box with this gift, it is not something that executives or the secretaries throw away. When accompanied by the gift, they typically read and pay more attention to the message(s) of your mailer, and they remember your company. Since this approach does cost more money than a normal mailing, it should be used for key target accounts. Even if it does cost $25 or more for each personalized gift, that's a small price to pay for a business relationship than can bring many thousands of dollars to your company.

- **Being Unique:** The personalized gift is one way of being unique. Following classical marketing principles and the UMS is another. Too many marketers do "me too" marketing. If your mailer is like everyone else's, it is more likely to be tossed in the trash. Through the headlines, words, pictures, graphics, shape of the brochure and a variety of other means, you have a lot of opportunity to stand out in the minds of the prospects who receive your mailing. The more unique, the better your positioning. The better your positioning, the more likely prospects will remember your company and products. If they remember you and think of you first, they are likely to buy from you when they are in the market for the kinds of products which you sell. Whatever you do with you mailer, think of being creative and unique in a classy and professional way.

FOLLOW THROUGH.

Unless your business is exclusively a catalog or mail order business, mailings will not close most of your sales. For that, you need sales people. The human touch is a very important part of the process of convincing prospects to buy your products. That's why it's a very good idea for sales people or telemarketing people to follow up on your direct mail efforts.

The other type of follow through is additional mailings. As mentioned previously, some experts believe that, for direct mail to work properly, each prospect should receive seven separate mailings spread over a reasonable period of time. There is no doubt that multiple mailings improve response rates. However, there should be a balance somewhere between getting your message to the customer and flooding him/her with too much "junk mail". Some people get annoyed when they continue to receive too much of the same thing over and over again. On the other hand, if the prospects are interested in your products, they won't be annoyed. Moreover, it's better to err on the "too much" side than the "too little" side. In many cases, prospects are not ready to buy during the first several mailings, but one of the later mailings might remind them of your products at a time when they are ready to buy in which case the mailing prompts them to take a buying action.

The last words on this subject are: One mailing won't do it; you have to follow through with several. The exact number will depend on many factors including your market, your company, and your budget.

POST CARDS AND CARD DECKS,

For Follow-up

A good way to be effective at the same time that you save money on your follow through is to use return reply post cards for subsequent mailings. Post cards are much less expensive to produce and mail than brochure-type mailers. More importantly, they serve to achieve the same results without annoying those who are tired of receiving the same mailing piece with each mailing. Many companies are finding that standard-sized (3.25" x 5.25") post cards with pictures of various company products are very popular with prospects. Each follow-up mailing could have a picture of a different product on it or the same product taken from different angles. Some companies are achieving considerable success by sending out post cards with works of art, scenic landscapes, and colorful graphics (which have nothing to do with the company or its products) on them.

For Primary Mailings

In addition to using post cards for "follow through" mailings, many companies have achieved success by using post cards as primary direct mail pieces. An example of this is shown in *Figure 13-4*. This type of post card can be enclosed with a personally typed letter on a first mailing, it can be given to a prospect at a trade show or seminar, or it can be sent in various follow-up mailings.

Card Decks

Another effective use of post cards is in the "card deck" mailings of various publications. These publications offer advertisers an alternative or adjunct to display ads whereby you can include your post card along with those of other firms (who may or may not be your competitors) in a card deck that is sent to the publication's subscription list. The card decks are usually wrapped in cellophane and sent to the entire list several times a year.

Ready Leads

Once prospects complete and return them, these post cards become ready qualified leads from which the sales people can take the appropriate follow-up action.

Reminders

Post cards can also be used very effectively to stay "in touch" with customers and prospects or to remind them of an appointment or a seminar. As always, even if they are used as reminders, a phone call should also be made as a final step in the reminder procedure.

Birthdays

Post cards make effective birthday cards. It's a "nice touch" for the marketing and/or sales department to send birthday post cards to customers, prospects, employees and people in various other important company publics. Most companies don't do this. That's why it's one good way for you to distinguish your company. Birthday information is available from so many different sources that it can be easily entered into company records.

POST CARD

COMPAL COMPUTER SYSTEMS

call COMPAL for
low-cost easy to use computer and
word processing systems for your business.

COMPAL, I am interested in:

- ☐ Word Processing
- ☐ Accounting
- ☐ Payroll
- ☐ Inventory
- ☐ Data Mgt.
- ☐ Real Estate
- ☐ Timekeeping & Billing
- ☐ Mailing
- ☐ Communications
- ☐ Other ____________

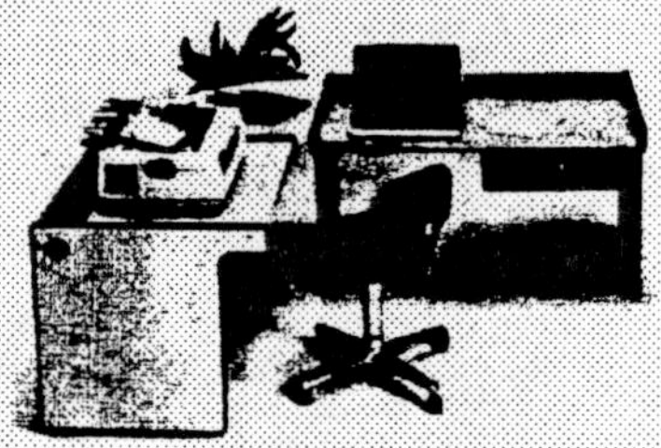

Name ____________________
Title ____________________
Company ____________________
Street ____________________
City ____________ State ____ Zip ______
Phone (Area Code) ____________________

☐ Please call me
☐ Send more information

COMPAL, INC. 8500 Wilshire Blvd., Beverly Hills, CA 90211 (213) 652-2263

No Postage
Necessary
If Mailed
In The
United States

BUSINESS REPLY MAIL
First Class Permit No. 627 Woodland Hills, CA U.S.A.

POSTAGE WILL BE PAID BY ADDRESSEE

COMPAL, INC.
6300 Variel Avenue, #E
Woodland Hills, CA 91367

Figure 13-4

Post Card Summary

In general, post cards can be a used with great success in your direct mail efforts. Whether used as a primary or follow-up direct mail piece, post cards are a very inexpensive way of effectively communicating with prospects and customers via the direct mail channel. Unlike other types of mailers, post cards do not have to possess a sophisticated, high-quality look. As with newsletters, prospects don't expect post cards to be "slick-looking". The information and the contact is more important.

It should be mentioned that high-quality post cards are not particularly expensive to produce. Photographic processes can be used which give post cards a quality-look for not much additional expense. As mentioned before, any quality put into the post card should done in such a way as to make the post card unique so that it will stand out in the minds of your prospects. Before being sent out, they should be personally signed along with a short hand-written note by the sales or marketing person assigned to the account or the company person who has most frequent contact with vendor or other public member.

PERSONAL LETTERS.

Although most people associate very large mass mailings with direct mail, personal letters should be included in every discussion of direct mail. Personal letters are one of the most effective methods of marketing to interested prospects. Once some contact is established with a prospect, the personal letter is a key tool in developing that all important personal relationship with the prospect. Unlike the more impersonal media ads and mailers, personal letters connect the sales and marketing people to the prospect. They complement telephone contact by giving sales and marketing personnel the opportunity to think over the concerns of the prospect and to formulate an intelligent response. They also provide a vehicle for communicating with prospects and customers in a way that is less interruptive than a phone call. That is, when you call prospects during a normal business day, they typically have to interrupt what they are doing to talk with you. When you send them a personal letter, they can choose a convenient time to read it, think about it and call you back.

If the sales people in your company have access to word processors for their letters, the marketing department should make "standard letters" available on these systems. These standard letters are pre-approved letters that sales people are authorized to send to their prospects and customers for a variety of purposes. Typical standard letters answer frequently raised objections; confirm appointments; thank prospects for their interest in company products; instruct customers on preparing their offices for delivery and installation of products; and respond to other requests. Sales personnel can personalize these letters so that they don't lose their personal flavor, and they should be encouraged to write customized letters for circumstances which are not covered by the standard letters. These customized letters, however, should be reviewed by an appropriate sales or marketing manager who is familiar with company policies, grammar, and communications techniques. This will "weed out" anything in these custom letters that might involve the company in litigation.

In whatever form, personalized letters are a very effective and inexpensive way of marketing a company's products and closing sales. While overlooked in too many companies, you should make them an institution in your organization.

SUMMARY.

Whether you have a large or small marketing budget, you can use direct mail to your great advantage in your marketing. There are two primary elements in direct mail — (1) the mailing piece which contains your message(s), and (2) the mailing list which includes your target prospects. The mailing piece should follow marketing principles and the UMS and should be unique so it will stand out from the crowd. Your mailing list is also critical to the success of your mailing. If you don't have a sufficiently large "home grown" list, you may need to rent or buy a mailing list to supplement your own list. Selecting the proper list involves matching the characteristics of people on the list with the profile of your market targets. Remember, you should expect a 1% return from a typical mailing. That means, if you need 100 qualified leads, you will need to send your mailing to 10,000 target prospects.

You can boost your mailing response with follow up. Follow up can and should be done with both subsequent mailings and phone follow-up. Post cards are good vehicles for follow-up mailings. They are inexpensive and effective, and they provide a way to avoid sending the same mailer to the same prospect over and over again. In addition to being good for follow-up, post cards are also good as inexpensive primary mailers, reminders, and birthday cards.

Once prospects have made some contact with your company, personal letters are a very effective and inexpensive form of direct mail. You should consider putting your collection of most effective letters used for various purposes in a "standard letters" file on your word processor. Sales people can personalize and send these pre-approved letters to their prospects and customers as needed. Those who are particularly effective writers should be encourage to send their own custom letters to prospects and customers after they have been reviewed by the appropriate authorities in sales or marketing.

SELECTED EXERCISES.

1. Contact key publications which your market targets read and other appropriate mailing list sources. Ask them to send you information on the mailing lists which they rent or sell.

2. Review the information and match it to your target market profiles.

3. Select the mailing list(s) which most accurately match your customer profiles.

4. Create a four or six-panel mailer for these target prospects. Refer to marketing principles, the UMS, and the information in this Chapter for reference.

5. Do the same as #4 in a standard 3.25" x 5.25" post card format.

Chapter 14 •CORPORATE IMAGE

"They make the first and sometimes last impressions on your publics..."

WHAT AFFECTS A COMPANY'S IMAGE?

Virtually everything your company does affects its image. Unfortunately, many companies forget this.

Image can be adversely affected by such transgressions as unreliable products, a company's involvement in politics or religion, socially unacceptable acts, layoffs, plant closings, bad publicity, disgruntled employees, unscrupulous competitors, bad service, long waits on the phone, "bad taste" signs and packaging, a bad name, cheap stationery, and impolite or uncooperative treatment of prospects and customers by employees.

Conversely, it can be helped by such positives as community assistance programs, public television and arts sponsorships, aid to universities and hospitals, donations to worthwhile causes, good treatment of various publics (customers, employees, etc.), a good name, good service (especially important with high-tech products), quality stationery, good-looking buildings and signage, plant tours, and congratulatory ads.

IT ALL STARTS WITH THE NAME.

Usually the first thing one learns about an organization is its name. Therefore, the selection of a name is a very important decision. A good name will create a good image consistent with an organization's line of business, might indicate the kind of business the firm is in, will be easily remembered, and will position a company properly relative to its competition. A not-so-good name may hurt a company's image and/or confuse its various publics. And name confusion can be very detrimental since it may diminish the return on the company's investment in marketing (i.e. dollars spent may be benefiting the other company whose name is the subject of the confusion). The confusion over Goodrich and Goodyear is a good example. Even worse, the other name, or names, with which it is confused may have negatives associated with it, or them.

Descriptive Names

Often the name of the founder or owner is used as part of the company name. While such a name can minimize the risks associated with ownership and infringing on trademarks, it can also have many disadvantages. Firstly, unless it is used in conjunction with other words that are descriptive of the business, it may be difficult for various publics to know what the firm does by reading its name. For example, if Hughes & Associates is the name of an aircraft firm, the name selection might be confusing. Is it a law firm? A consulting firm? An ad agency? Or what? Hughes Aircraft is better. Secondly, using a personal name can cause needless customer fears. One of the many concerns customers have with companies (particularly high-tech companies) is the fear they'll go out of business and not be around to support and service their products. In today's marketplace, using a personal name for a new company often fuels such fears since a personal name normally implies the firm is small and/or a "mom and pop" family business. Small implies less stable since many small companies find difficulty surviving against much larger competition. That is, when the going gets tough, the tough go surfing in Hawaii. Thirdly, its more difficult to establish useful graphic images and positions in the minds of prospects with personal names. In addition, some prospects may know someone they don't like with the same or similar name and have a negative image of the company as a result.

Names for New Companies

For new companies, an effective name should create images of something unique and better than existing companies in the same industry. If possible, it should also give an indication of the type of business or industry the company is in, and/or it should be descriptive of the type of products the company sells.

Good Choice

Several years ago, a new company that specializes in making portable computers selected the name Compaq. It's an effective name because its brief (two syllables), implies computers with the prefix "Comp" and creates an image of portability with a name that sounds like compact. As of this writing, Compaq has been a phenomenal success in a very competitive industry and has made significant inroads in the PC market against very stiff competition from IBM and Apple. In addition to a good name, it populated much of its executive ranks with seasoned marketing and sales executives from IBM.

A Name that Causes Difficulties Later

Apple is a personal computer company that built its success in the education and computer hobby market. In this market, its name has served it very well. It has had considerably more difficulty, however, penetrating the Fortune 1000 market. Many of the decision makers in these large companies have associated the name "Apple" with education or fun and games and not with serious business computing. While Apple's loyal following and excellent products have begun to overcome the purchasing resistance caused by the name and its associated image, the company has lost a significant number of sales and market share to IBM, Compaq and others, in no small part, because of the image created by the name.

How to Choose a Good Name

Make a list of successful names. When selecting a name, a useful first step is to write down the names of successful companies and products which you admire. This list should include companies and products both inside and outside of your industry. Such company names as *Coca-Cola, IBM, Kodak, General Motors, Sears, McDonalds, Xerox, Hertz, Hilton Hotels, Chase Manhattan Bank, American Express, Procter & Gamble, Arthur Andersen, and CBS* may or may not be on your list. As for product names, you might have identified the *Macintosh computer, Ford Mustang, Cannon "Sureshot" Cam-*

era, *TRW Credit Services, Numero Uno Pizza, Time Magazine, or the Burger King "Whopper" Hamburger.*

Identify why they are successful. Next, ask yourself why these names have come to represent very successful companies and products. Some reasons might include the names are: historical, first into your mind, simple, descriptive of the product or industry, easy to remember, catchy, heavily promoted, pervasive, representative, symbolic, substantial sounding, and comfortable. Analyzing the reasons should do at least two things for you — (1) help to trigger ideas for your names and (2) give you an idea as to what makes an effective name.

Understand the psychological aspect of names. In doing your analyses and creating your own names, you should understand that names have a psychological as well as descriptive component. Names that begin with hard consonant sounds or use words that have connotations of size, substance, or power connote images of strength, security and longevity. Examples include: Kodak, Polaroid, Coca-Cola, Bold detergent, Dodge Charger, and International Business Machines. On the other hand, names that are soft sounding connote delicacy and gentleness. Examples include: Faberge perfume, Jean Naté bath oil, Charmin bathroom tissue, and Ivory soap.

Create your own list. The next step is for you to create a list of names for your company and/or products. If brilliant names don't come to you immediately, write down the prefixes and suffixes of the successful names identified above, and mix and match them to form new names. Be careful, however, not to create names which can be easily confused with the names from which you obtained the prefixes and suffixes. Remember, you usually want your name to stand out and be remembered in a positive context.

For example, there are lots of standard prefixes and suffixes used in high-tech names that can be combined to formulate new names — i.e. *Com, Comp, Digi, Data, Elec, Quan, Memory, Mem, mation, tron, ix, ics, ex, rex, rox, on, ec, ic, in, al, tel, el, com, storage, ...*

Narrow the list to a few top choices. You should think about the advantages and disadvantages of using the selected names to represent your company or products. Advantages should be similar to those identified in your analysis of successful names above. Don't forget the image, or psychological aspects.

Test the names on others who are objective. Once several potentially "good" names are selected, they should be tested (i.e. do some Market Research). There is no need to hire some expensive research firm to do this. One can ask friends, business associates, prospects, customers (if the company is a going concern), vendors, and even competitors. However, make sure that you do the test objectively. If you give them any indication as to the names you prefer, you are likely to bias their answers. It's best to give them a list in alphabetical order, and to ask them to give their opinions as to which names they like the best. They're in a more objective position to evaluate the name than the founders who created it. What these objective sources have to say should be seriously considered against the more subjective instincts of the top executives of the organization. The greatest weight should be given to the opinions of customers and prospects since they are the ones who will be buying.

Do a name search to avoid conflicts. The final selection(s) should then be scrutinized against a search of other names in the same industry. The objective is to make sure that the name does not conflict with other trademarked names being used for similar products. This can be done by going to the library, by hiring a search firm, using an in-house attorney, or an outside legal counsel. The outside lawyer will probably be the most expensive and will most likely hire a search firm to do a computer search anyway. A patent attorney should be used if the firm intends to formally trademark the name that has been selected. In any event, the newly selected name can be protected by having an article or a notice published establishing the date the name is first used. Also, use in interstate commerce can help to protect the name of products sold beyond state lines. Until such time as a trademark is registered, all uses of the name selected should have a "TM" as a superscript following the name. If and when the trademark is officially registered, the name will be followed by a superscripted "R in a circle" — [®]. After getting a trademark registered, however, it can be lost if the name becomes too generic, the company does not challenge uses that fail to affix the registration notice, or the name is challenged in court. Examples of the former include trade-marked names that have been used generically such as Kleenex and Xerox. An example of the latter is a challenge brought by *Minnesota Mining and Manufacturing,* which uses the mark *3M,* against a then new company named *Electronic Memories* which used the mark *EM* (they are now *Electronic Memories and Magnetics,* or *EMM).* 3M claimed that EM was too close and would confuse 3M's publics. EM hired an ophthalmologist as an expert witness who testified that even people with impaired vision would not confuse the two. EM won the case.

Measure results. As with all marketing decisions, you should measure the results of your name choices. Make sure that the sales, support and service people who typically interface with customers take note of any positive or negative comments about the company or product names. These comments should be put in writing and given to the marketing executives for evaluation. While name changes should not be made lightly, you should consider making changes if names are causing consistently negative associations with your company or any of its products.

An over-the-counter diet product named AYDS was recently changed as a result of its sounding exactly like the acronym for the dreaded disease Acquired Immune Deficiency Syndrome (AIDS). Initially, the company didn't want to change the product name. However, its decline in sales and subsequent market research indicated that a name change is in order.

LOGOS.

In conjunction with the name, it is important to think about a logo and stationery. These are the next items that a company's publics will typically see. Because they will have a profound affect on the company's image, they represent two important marketing decisions. Unless a talented and creative designer is on staff, this is an area where a company might want to seek outside professional help. The best way to find firms who specialize in logo and stationery design is to either go through the company's ad agency (if it has a good one) or to find examples of good-looking logos/stationery and ask the companies who use them for the firms who created the designs. Once this list is compiled, the firms identified should be interviewed in regard to their fees and their understanding of the company's industry and products.

Before making a final selection, one should make sure that the designers will offer several alternatives from which to choose. If possible, one should get the designer to quote a fixed fee for the project. If the budget for this is very limited, one way to obtain professional designs at a very low cost is to sponsor a competition amongst students of a respected design school nearby. Who knows? It's possible that the winner might be a candidate for employment some day. In any event, once the alternatives are designed, it is necessary to test their acceptance amongst the company's publics (more Market Research). Again objectivity is the key, and it is best to find a sample that most closely approximates the company's prospects and customers.

Think of the logo as a stamp that will stamp an image of your company in the minds of your publics. Remember, it will appear on stationery, business cards, signs, brochures, packages, and products. Therefore, it is important. Along with the name, it will serve to create an image and a position for your company and products in the minds of your publics.

Designing your own logo

Before hiring an outside firm to design your logo, you might want to try to do it yourself. If the results are not effective, you can always go to an outside specialist. If you have a sophisticated computer or desk top publishing system, your task will be much easier. There are several capable software programs which assist you in creating logos. A phone call to a computer dealer or software distributor who carries desktop publishing systems and software might be a good place to find the one that is most appropriate for you. Additionally, there are public domain clip art libraries on computer disks which might provide you with elements or ideas which you can use in creating your logo.

Sources of ideas

There are many sources of ideas for your logo. Some include:

Graphic representation of the product. *Figure 14-1* shows a logo for a portable computer product from Compal called the Electric Briefcase. The product logo is a graphical representation of a briefcase.

Initials. A common source of logos is the initials of the company name. *Figure 14-2* shows an example of an "initials" logo for *Kalb & Associates*. The "K" was created to communicate several concepts about the firm including its professionalism and specialization in high-tech industries.

Symbol formed by initials. In addition to using initials, some logos are formed by creating unique symbols from the company's initials. *Figure 14-3* shows a Dataproducts logo which is the result of this technique.

Representation of the product function. *Figure 14-4* shows the logo of *Southern California Edison*, an electric utility company. The company initials in the logo are cleverly designed as a graphical representation of an electric wire and plug — symbols of the electric service provided by the company.

Product example used as company logo. Some companies are so closely identified with one of their products that they use this product in their corporate logo. *Disney* is a good example. They uses *Mickey Mouse* in their corporate logo.

Symbol to create an image. Some companies have symbols created to reflect an image they want the company to project. *Figure 14-5* shows at *AT&T* logo which is a high-tech version of a globe. This logo communicates something about the global nature of the company's high-tech products and services.

Graphically-interesting Shapes. Some logos are created from geometric or other interesting shapes which may or may not have something to do with the company's business. These shapes are used to be attractive symbols which will be easily remembered and positively associated with the company.

GRAPHIC OF PRODUCT LOGO

Electric
Briefcase™

Figure 14-1

INITIALS LOGO

KALB & ASSOCIATES

Figure 14-2

INITIALS SYMBOL LOGO

Figure 14-3

SERVICE SYMBOL LOGO

Figure 14-4

IMAGE CREATION LOGO

Figure 14-5

These are just some examples of sources for logo ideas. They should serve to help you generate ideas for your company and product logos.

Design Considerations

Since the logo is a very important symbol to your company, you should consider the possible uses of the logo in your design.

How will it look when reproduced? Many logos that incorporate multiple colors look great on an original document, but lose their effectiveness when they are copied. The multi-colored logo of *Apple Computer* is such an example. Multiple colors are not the only "things" that cause problems upon reproduction. Logos which use elements that are shaded, three dimensional, or formed by closely spaced lines also deteriorate when copied. To avoid the reproduction problem in newspaper ads, Apple Computer does have a solid black version of its logo. However, this still doesn't solve the problems created when letterhead and other items with the multi-colored logo are copied using a copy machine.

What effects will colors have? Colors have symbolic meanings to many cultures outside the United States — especially to those in the Far East. For example green symbolizes sickness and death in certain Asian countries. The use of a particular color in a logo can adversely affect the success of the product and company in certain countries.

In additional to cultural considerations, some colors are considered trendy. Use of such colors will adversely affect the product and company when they lose favor with the public. The pastel pinks and greens commonly referred to as "Miami Vice" colors (after the TV show of the same name) are one example of trendy colors which are have begun to fall out of favor with many buyers.

Colors also may or may not be considered appropriate for certain types of products. Cool and high-contrast colors are considered appropriate for high-tech or modern looking products. Warm earth and wood tones are used for such products as wood furniture, gardening products, and pottery.
In general, colors fall in and out of style. Therefore, there are two

basic choices when selecting colors for a logo. Change colors as styles change or use colors that don't go in and out of style. Black and white (including certain shades of gray) are the safest, with certain shades of blue and red also being a safe choice.

Letter styles and shapes. As with colors, certain letter styles are considered trendy and should be avoided unless the product is going to be a fad item or the company is willing to make changes as styles change.

Sometimes logos are changed to give a company a new and fresh outlook. *United Airlines* changed their logo years ago because they felt the old logo used lettering that was becoming out of fashion. They felt that an airline company should have an innovative and up-to-date image rather than one grounded in tradition. The public agreed with them since the logo has become widely accepted over the years with a minimum of customer resistance.

There are cases where the public does not agree with a logo or label change. In early 1989, *Coors* tried to change their logo and label design to a more modern, high-tech style. As a result of this change, beer sales immediately dropped and many customers complained about the new label. This caused Coors to change back to the old design.

Numbers. As with letters and colors, shapes and numbers have different connotations to different peoples and cultures. In many American circles, the number 13 is considered bad luck. In Japan, the number "4" means death. Therefore, it's not a good idea to include the number four in the name or logo of any products which are to be exported to Japan. For example, the *Basic Four* computer and *4-Way cold tablets* would have a tough time penetrating the Japanese market.

Protection

Once you create a good logo, you should protect it so that nobody else can legally copy it for their own purposes. As with names, logo's can be trademarked. Until such time as you decide to register the trademark (at which time you will super-script the logo with an ®), you can put a ™ as a superscript trailing the first use of the logo in each publication.

Uses of logos

Your company logo should appear on virtually all of your company materials including ads, brochures, stationery, business cards, newsletters, product packages, shipping labels, invoices and other documents.

STATIONERY.

The term "stationery" typically refers to letterhead, "2nd page" stationery (for all pages after the 1st), envelopes and business cards.

Letterhead

The first page of a letter which contains information about the company is called letterhead.

What should be printed on letterhead? Letterhead should contain the following: company logo, the company name (if it's not already part of the logo), statement of the company's business (if not already obvious), address, phone number, and fax (and/or telex) number. Since most of your personal correspondence is going to be presented on your letterhead, it should portray the very best image possible.

Factors which affect the quality of the letterhead? The quality of letterhead is derived from many different factors such as:

- *Paper quality.* The more cotton content the better the quality.

- *The design of the letterhead.* A clean and professional-looking design is the best. This is another case where less is more.

- *Printing technique.* The best quality letterhead has information engraved or printed with a top-quality press.

- *Ink quality and color.* If printing with ink is chosen over engraving, the ink quality and color are important. The ink color will depend on the type of business and the industry. Businesses where conservatism is required should play it safe with conservative shades of black, gray or blue.

Placement of the elements on the letterhead page

The logo and the company name should be placed at the top of the letterhead. They can be left justified, centered or right justified. Left justified is the most popular and most practical since it allows for greater typing area. The company business statement or slogan should appear underneath or alongside the logo and company name. The address, phone, fax and other information can either be placed at the top or bottom of the letterhead. Many prefer stringing this information along the bottom of the page since it is a "dead" area for typing, and it serves to help frame the text on the page. *Figure 14-6* shows an example of letterhead with address and phone information at the bottom.

The second page

Subsequent pages are typically blank versions of the letterhead. That is, they use the same paper, and they have nothing printed on them. In rare cases, companies use different paper for subsequent pages. Some even have information printed on them. However, these cases represent the exception rather than the rule. In your effort to create a unique image, anything is possible as long you have assured yourself that such uniqueness will not have adverse effects on the company's image.

Envelopes

The envelopes should be coordinated with the stationery. In general, they should incorporate the following:

Logo and company name. The company name and logo should appear on the envelope. Due to postal conventions for placement of the return address, the choice is basically between the upper left corner and the back flap. Most businesses choose to put their return address on the front since it will be better seen by all in the postal chain.

Positioning statement or slogan. Organizations should put

LETTERHEAD

Figure 14-6

a *positioning statement* or slogan on the envelope. This "tells the world" the company's line of business or some other unique and distinguishing characteristic about the organization. It is an promotional opportunity to make a positive impression on the minds of mail handlers and recipients (whether or not they open the envelope). This positioning statement often appears beneath the company name, but is sometimes placed at the bottom left or right of the envelope or on the back flap.

Return address. The return address almost always appears with the logo and company name in the upper left corner of the front or on the back flap.

Other items. The envelope may also be adorned with graphic lines, decorations, or other items. In certain businesses, instructions on how to make payment or reminders to include such information as account numbers on checks is printed somewhere on the back of the envelope.

Figure 14-7 shows an example of an envelope for Compal Computers.

Business Cards

Business cards should contain much the same information as company stationery plus two other very important items — individual name and title. Since the business card is a calling card that will be given or mailed to many different publics, its design should not be taken lightly. Whereas a statement about the company's business is optional on letterhead and envelopes, it should be included on business cards (unless there is some very strong reason not to include it). The reason for this is that many business cards are exchanged at trade shows and business meetings. Too often, people forget to write important notes on them. Therefore, unless the type of business is represented on the card, most people are likely to forget what your company does.

Unfortunately, with business cards, there are few standards as to the location of information on the card. To achieve proper design balance, important information should be arranged so it can be easily read and understood and looks graphically pleasing. To give you some reference to follow, there are two

ENVELOPE

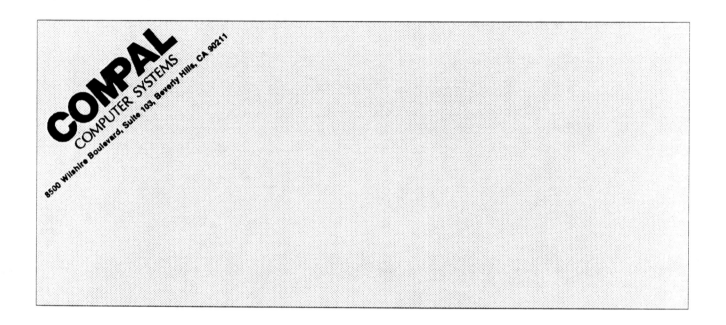

Figure 14-7

basic designs which are most popular. They both involve orienting the card in the horizontal (landscape) direction. The first puts the logo, or some other single element, on one side of the card (usually the left) and all of the other information (name, title, address, phone and fax) lined up on the other. Examples of this style include *IBM, Wang,* and *AT&T.* The second centers the information in the middle of the card. A popular variation of this design is to center a focal element such as name and title or the company logo and to put the remaining information below on both the left and right. Many law, consulting and accounting firms use this design. *Figure 14-8* shows a business card example for *Kalb & Associates.*

General Design Considerations

In addition to containing the information enumerated above, letterhead, envelopes and business cards should reflect the following design considerations:

Size. You should probably not use size as one of the ways to distinguish your company. Many of the printers, copy machines and other automated devices in your office rely on your use of standard-size paper. Postal authorities are also becoming more and more automated and are requiring standard-size envelopes to qualify for standard postal rates. As for business cards, most of the business card holders and files are designed for a standard size.

Texture. When selecting paper stock for your stationery, you should consider how your letterhead and business cards are likely to be used. Customers and prospects often need to write notes on them. Therefore, using onion skin paper for your letterhead or super glossy stock for your business cards is probably not a good idea. Heavily-grained paper may have a "rich" look to some, but it creates havoc when used in laser printers. In addition to jamming the printer more frequently, the toner used by most laser printers is not easily fused to grainy paper. As a result, the printed words often disintegrate where the stationery paper is folded.

Quality. Although mentioned before, paper quality is something which marketers should be reminded of frequently. It plays a very important role in presenting a quality image of your

BUSINESS CARD

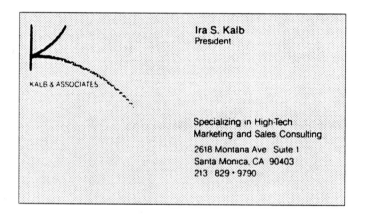

Figure 14-8

organization. In addition to looking and feeling better, quality paper holds ink and folds better. It also holds up better under normal handling. You should select a paper which has some "rag" or cotton content. A 25% cotton-content paper is not much more expensive than a lesser quality paper. You can make up the difference in cost by purchasing your paper from a paper wholesaler in your area rather than through your printer or ad agency.

Balance. The layout of information on stationery is very important. An amateurish design will be out of balance. It's like viewing a painting or photograph which has elements located in places which don't look or "feel" right. All elements on the business card, letterhead and envelope should be uncluttered and in balance. Following the rules of the UMS should help, but letterhead needs to achieve balance at the same time as it leaves sufficient room for typed text. Also, the final balance can only be achieved when text is printed on it. That's why so many big corporations, such as IBM, have specific guidelines for formatting letters. Business cards need to pack a lot of information in a small amount of space. As discussed in the Section on the "Non-linearity of Space and Time", the proper layout will look uncluttered even if a lot of information is placed close together, whereas a poor layout will look cluttered when there is a lot of room to spare.

What factors create proper balance and harmony? The location and sizing of various elements so they can be easily read, they are visually appealing, they work together (rather than fight with each other) and they are distinctive enough to stand out from the crowd (in a positive context) when thumbing through a pile of cards or letterheads in a file.

OTHER CORPORATE IMAGE PIECES.

Since virtually everything affects a company's image, there are many other pieces which could be discussed. Any attempts to cover all of them, however, would be impractical. It would require many volumes and would involve too much repetition of the same concepts and principles. It would violate the marketing principle of *positioning* whereby the most important points would be lost in the clutter. Company signage, product packaging, business forms, and office design are just a few of the more important ones. Anyway, the concepts and techniques discussed above in regard to logos and stationery are quite applicable to the creation of these marketing vehicles.

There are two other items that should be discussed since they can greatly help the marketing of the corporate image yet they are largely ignored by many companies. They both contain similar information, and both should be located in the company's lobby. The first is the Publicity Book. The second is the permanent framing and displaying of important publicity.

Publicity Book

The *Publicity Book* should contain a chronological (or other logical) record of publicity on the company. The information in this book should include the following:

- *Articles* written about the company, its products and personnel.
- *Testimonial letters* (also known as *fan* letters) from customers and other publics.
- *Articles* written by company employees.
- *References* to community relation's efforts sponsored by the company.
- *Honors and awards* bestowed upon the *company, its products and personnel.*
- *Publicity, honors and awards* bestowed upon *key customers.*

As new publicity is discovered or received, it should be added to the Book. Receptionists should invite prospects and other publics to review the *Publicity Book* while they are waiting for an appointment.

Sales handouts and mailers

Sales people should be given access to duplicate copies of good publicity for use in their sales calls and demonstrations. They should also be encouraged to send reprints to prospects and customers. If properly presented, the *Publicity Book* can do wonders for the image of the company and its products. It can also help to move interested prospects closer to taking buying actions by making them feel more comfortable with the company and its products.

Training

All personnel should be presented with good publicity as part of their training and orientation to the organization. This will tend to confirm their choice to join the company and will start their employment relationship *on the right foot.*

Framed Publicity

Many corporate lobbies have attractive works of art, but no framed examples of company publicity. Important publicity and awards should be professionally framed and hung in the lobby and key visitor-traveled corridors of the company. These will serve to impress visitors and inspire them to take buying actions or spread the word to others about your company and products. They will attract the attention of those who don't have the opportunity to review the Publicity Book, and they will reinforce the messages to those who do. If you're a record company, nothing will impress your visitors quicker than Gold or Platinum Records hanging on the walls. If you're an ad agency, the Obie awards will have the same effect. For other industries, many other forms of recognition that are nicely framed and hung on the walls will perform more "magic" for the company than most other forms of marketing. What's more, it's free. The only "out-of-pocket" cost is the cost of the framing.

If there is any extra space on your walls after your publicity and awards, you should similarly frame your most effective ads. They will serve to show your publics that you are a substantial company who regularly advertises in top-level publications. The messages of the framed ads will reach those who've never seen them before, and fortify the effect on those who have.

CONCLUSION.

Understanding the importance of maintaining a positive corporate image and remaining continually aware of the factors which affect image, will put you ahead of most marketers. While this is easy to comprehend, it's hard to remember — particularly during the "heat of battle" characteristic of most business environments. The following list should help.

1. Virtually everything a company and its employees do affect its image.

2. Everyone in a company should be made aware of this fact.

3. A company, through its marketing and behavior, must do whatever possible to consciously maintain a good image in the minds of all its publics.

4. Members of all publics should be looked upon and treated as if they were unpaid ambassadors and sales people of the company.

5. Every person in the company should be trained to be conscious of the factors that affect its image, and should counteract any negatives that could serve to tarnish that image.

6. Any actions which damage the image of a company should be dealt with quickly, honestly, and decisively.

7. A concerted effort should be made to turn negatives into positives, not with just words, but with follow-up actions and effective marketing pieces.

The selection of names, design of logos and stationery, and the development of many other corporate image pieces play a big role in formulating company and product images. The biggest role, however, is played by the positive attitudes and actions of top management and the successful transferal of these attitudes and actions to other company employees. With the proper attitude, the resultant commitment and a little talent, the company's corporate image will be secure.

SELECTED EXERCISES.

1. Collect a piece of letterhead and a business card from a successful company whose stationery you admire.

2. Compare their stationery to your company's. Note any differences.

3. Redesign the letterhead and business card in light of your comparison above.

4. Create a name for a new product or rename an existing product using the criteria discussed in this Chapter.

5. Collect company publicity and put together a Publicity Book for your company lobby(ies). Consider framing and displaying the most impressive examples.

Notes.

Chapter 15: WORD OF MOUTH

"It can be your most effective form of advertising..."

WHAT IS IT?

Word-of-mouth advertising refers to the process whereby members of your various publics verbally spread information about your company and products from one person to another. It is of critical importance to professional service firms (such as law, medical, accounting, and consulting firms) who, because of historical taboos, do not typically advertise in conventional ways. Many of these professional firms rely almost exclusively on word-of-mouth advertising. While most companies in other industries are not subject to such taboos, virtually all of them find that positive word-of-mouth advertising is a critical element in their success. Because of its universal importance, this subject has been given its own chapter in this book.

WHY IS IT SO IMPORTANT?

The information that is passed from person to person can be good or bad. If it's good, it can be your must effective form of advertising. If it's bad, it can be devastating to your business. According to the Wall Street Journal on Marketing, studies show that only 4 percent of dissatisfied customers complain directly to a company about its products. The other 96 percent (the "silent majority") stop buying the product, and also bad-mouth it to 9 or 10 other people. In contrast, complaints that are quickly resolved, lead to repeat purchases in 82 to 95 percent of the cases. Moreover, customers whose complaints are answered and satisfied pass the positive word to at least 5 other people within 10 days.

As a result of its importance, you might assume that most companies direct most of their marketing efforts into promoting positive word-of-mouth advertising. In actuality, the opposite is true. Most companies neglect this subject completely. If they are aware of the concept at all, they assume that it is something which follows its own course and which is outside the realm of the their control. The very successful companies not only understand its importance, they take definitive steps to promote positive word-of-mouth advertising.

WHAT STEPS CAN BE TAKEN?

Corporate Image

As already discussed in the previous Chapter on "Corporate Image Pieces", everything a company does affects its image. Promoting a strong positive image is a necessary prerequisite for word-of-mouth success. All of the corporate image pieces previously discussed contribute to this process.

Good Service

The first step in getting referrals is to spoil customers. Give customers such good service that they will tell their associates and friends without solicitation. Included in the company's efforts to deliver good service should be marketing pieces which query the customer as to their satisfaction with the company's products. This "query" often takes different forms. It can be in the form of a question at the bottom of a sales invoice or a restaurant bill which solicits a customer response; or it can be part of a warranty card which the customer mails in to register for warranty service. It can even be a separate short questionnaire which solicits customer opinions about the product. Merely having these pieces, however, will not insure good service. They have to be accompanied by the company policy and commitment to deliver good service.

Rewards

The next step is to reward customers for referrals that turn into good prospects and sales. The reward should not be in the form of a "bribe" or commission. This is likely to backfire and cause "image damage" since reputable people and companies don't offer bribes or "kick backs". The reward should be in the form of a discount on future product purchases, a thank you note, or a phone call. An invitation to lunch or dinner is another positive way of thanking the customer for a referral. The lunch or dinner can serve another positive purpose. It can give you important intelligence information on what the customer wants as well as what the customer likes and doesn't like about your products. To collect this information and provide it to marketing decision makers, the salesperson who takes the customer to lunch should be instructed to complete a Market Information Form. See *Figure 15-1.*

Incentives

Unlike a bribe or a kick back, an incentive is a bonus that is publicized to all customers and earned. That is, it is similar to "frequent flyer" awards offered by the airlines or to a free wash for every 10 car washes that are paid. To make extra sure that customers don't misinterpret such incentives, you should be very careful in wording and publicizing them. For example, acceptable wording might be as follows: "As a special New Year's thank you, we are offering two tickets to the hit show 'Phantom of the Opera' to all customers whose referrals purchase one of our sofas by the end of December." Notice, this incentive is offered to all customers and it is not excessive. Large incentives may backfire since some prospects might think that their associates only recommended your products because of the incentive offered.

Testimonials

Whenever customers say nice "things" about the company's products, you should ask them if they wouldn't mind putting their words in writing and sending them to you in a letter. For each testimonial, you should have them sign a legal release which allows the company to quote them in its marketing pieces. An example of such a release was shown in Figure 8-2 of Chapter 8.

Since most people like to receive positive recognition, the publication of the customer's case history or testimonial will

No. 419

KALB & ASSOCIATES • Market Information Form

Specializing in High-technology Marketing • Sales • Systems Consulting and Training

> INSTRUCTIONS — PLEASE READ FIRST. Continued success of our company requires the on-going assistance of everyone in our organization (the company's "eyes and ears") to provide marketplace information on a timely basis. Whenever you are able to collect such information please complete this form and send it to the marketing department. Bonuses will be awarded to the top submissions, and performance reviews will reflect your efforts. Thank you.

Type of Information — ☐ New product ideas ☐ Competition ☐ Compliment
☐ Complaint ☐ Strategy feedback ☐ Other_____

Source of Information

Name		Date		

Position	Phone

Company	Fax

Street	P.O. Box

City	State	Zip

Employee Reporting

Name	Position	Department	Phone Extension

Market Information (Please write on back or attach a separate sheet if necessary.)

_____

_____

_____

_____

_____

_____

_____

_____

_____

The following signature releases the company from any obligations or liabilities associated with using the above information for its marketing or other purposes.

Signature	Title	Date

Form No. K&A 081492 • Last Revision 9/30/92   **Please send to Marketing Department when completed.**

Figure 15-1

serve to strengthen your bond with that customer and to "turn that customer on" to playing a more active role in referring business to your company. It also has a positive affect on those prospects who know and trust that customer. Additionally, those prospects who don't even know the featured customer are likely to be positively influenced by the case history. It shows them fact that there is someone, just like them, who is happy with your company's products. *Figure 15-2* provides an example of a customer testimonial in the form of a case history hand out. Newsletters, brochures, and display ads are also good formats for customer testimonials and case histories.

Phone Messages

In an effort to entertain callers while they wait to speak with an employee who is not immediately available, many companies have gone to a system which plays music while callers are on hold. While many don't believe this to be an important marketing decision, it is a marketing decision that affects the company's image nonetheless. In fact, studies have shown that some callers really get annoyed if they don't like the music being played.

Some companies have even chosen to play commercials while callers are on hold.

Many companies are going to a "phone mail" type of system whereby callers are greeted with personal phone messages if the party being called is not available. After hearing the outgoing message, the caller can then leave a personal message much the same as on a personal answer machine.

As to which method is preferred, "school is still out". The phone mail system seems to be the least offensive, but marketing personnel will have to sample the opinions of callers to find out which works best for their particular company.

Office Design and Layout

While some companies are unconcerned with the look of their offices, it does make an impression on the company's various publics. Even though significant numbers of people don't possess "good taste", most can recognize aesthetically pleasing

COMPAL *CASE HISTORY*

MIKE HANSEN, Businessman

Mike Hansen bought his computer system principally for his own convenience, to ease the bookkeeping and billing chores of his small business. ("I'm no paperwork buff – I'm a burglar alarm installer.") As things are working out, he winds up also with sharply stepped-up service to his customers, and beyond that with a whole new business enterprise in which the computer itself becomes a profit center.

Hansen Alarm Company provides security services to some 200 accounts, each covered for any of several "zones" of concern – burglary, fire, medical emergency, and so on. Detection devices at each location transmit coded signals when help is needed. The signals are monitored and analyzed for source and zone. In response, calls go out to police and other functionaries, to the customer, and to Mike himself, who makes it a practice to follow such calls if only to protect his own equipment. All the gear is routinely or specially maintained, repaired, and upgraded/replaced. Accidental signals and false alarms must be identified and planned against, sometimes charged for. . . All activity must go into the record, and each month, of course, must be sorted out: each of the 200 accounts billed for standard and extraordinary services, with appropriate notification of contract expiration dates, late payments and other matters. . . So paperwork was mighty onerous to Mike's tightly-knit operation.

Always alert to technical developments, Mike decided in 1976 that the newly-arrived microcomputer ought to be able to help him, and started shopping for equipment. He finally found at Compal what nobody else was offering: a complete, matched-up system ready to plug in and go to work. ("It's still that way. Nobody else does what Compal does, taking responsibility for the whole thing.")

With Compal's guidance, Mike settled on a 32K Compal-80

with cassette and dual disk drives, small keyboard, large CRT, and a DECwriter. . . and studied programming in our classes. His investment was about $7000. ("Friend of mine in the business bought himself a different make of computer at the same time, paid $40,000 for it. He laughed at me and my Compal outfit.")

In short order, Mike had achieved his objective. Armed with some of Compal's business programming plus some Mike himself built for the special needs of his alarm company, the Compal system took over: storing all account data, then each month collating and calculating, addressing and printing fully-documented invoices, flagging significant contract and payment information – altogether letting technology carry the burden of the irksome chores, as it should. (As Edison said, "If your sewing machine doesn't have an electric motor, you're working for three cents an hour.")

Now Mike has tied in his Compal system with the monitored signals from his alarms. A four-digit code calls up from memory a display of all relevant data, so that response now starts in seconds – a noticeable speed-up over previous methods, and so a recognizable benefit to Hansen Alarm subscribers. Beyond that: with systems running and computer capacity to spare, Mike has established CASS Computer Assisted Security Service, Inc. – providing to other Southern California alarm companies the service he set up for himself.

"Oh yes, about my friend with the $40,000 machine? He still hasn't got that thing running for him! And mine – even with another dual drive and some extra memory added, I'm still well under $10,000, and I can do anything he'll be able to do if he ever does get it going."

Success story in the classic mold: Microcomputer saves work, improves service, brings new profits. . . and gets the last laugh.

Figure 15-2

surroundings when they see them. Buyers like to visit "nice places" and employees seem to like to work longer in surroundings which are pleasant. Because if its importance to a company's image, consideration should be given to the look of the office as part of the firm's promotional strategies.

Signage

Signs are an important identifier of a company's location. Those that are aesthetically pleasing contribute to the company's image, while those that are not cause some people to question other "things" about the company. In addition to looking good, signs should be visible and make an impact. Even those prospects who walk or drive by are affected by signs which they see. Every time they see the sign, the company's name and logo are recorded in their minds. Whenever they see an ad, receive a mailer, or are called upon by a company sales person, they will be more receptive and comfortable because the name on the sign will already be in their mind.

People contacts

One of the easiest ways of promoting positive word-of-mouth advertising about your company and products is to look at every contact with customers, prospects, and other members of your various publics as an opportunity to make a friend. To achieve this end, you should make sure that you have policies and procedures delineated in a Policy and Procedures manual (written by marketers) to guide your personnel as to how to properly handle these contacts.

When people call on the phone, their call should be answered promptly. Up to five rings is acceptable. The person answering the phone should identify the company and perhaps add their own name followed by words such as, "May I help you?" No matter who the callers are or what they say, they should be properly treated. This is sometimes hard to do with rude and/ or overly aggressive callers. The phone answerer should be trained to anticipate such calls and to react in a positive and constructive manner.

When people walk into your company locations, they should be treated in the same professional and courteous manner. They should be offered coffee or some other available beverage, and they shouldn't be made to wait very long.

Phone messages should be returned promptly. If the target of the phone message is out of town or too busy, another employee should be trained to respond.

Letters to the company should be routed to the proper person for a response, and a written and/or verbal response should follow promptly.

Complaints should not be looked upon as personal challenges. They should be viewed as opportunities to turn negatives into positives. Even if the phone, walk-in and letter contacts are obnoxious or discourteous, the person who responds should do so in a professional and understanding manner. Sometimes customers and other members of publics have a right to be angry. Other times they don't. Whatever the case, your only chance for turning this person around to being a positive word-of-mouth advertiser is to answer their complaint and treat them with all the courtesy and professionalism you can muster.

One company who does an outstanding job of handling contacts with publics is Microsoft, the software company from Bellevue, Washington. Another company that does a good job is IBM. It's no wonder that both of these companies are leaders in their respective industries.

CONCLUSION.

In general, taking care of your customers and your other publics will bring you positive results. Failing to take care of them will bring the opposite. All members of your company's publics should be looked upon as ambassadors and unpaid sales people for your company. Every marketing piece you create to help you in your efforts will enhance your company's image which will, in turn, bring you many more sales. As discussed in the beginning of this Chapter, good news travels fast, but bad news travels faster. More importantly, bad feelings can be turned into good feelings which can be transformed into "free" positive word-of-mouth advertising. In order to do this, everyone in the company has to be trained to look at negatives and complaints as opportunities to turn people around and to develop a closer relationship with them. The company's *Policy and Procedures* manual is the marketing piece which can guide you in the proper direction in this regard. The other marketing pieces discussed in this Chapter can also play a major role in actively soliciting positive word-of-mouth advertising. However, what's written on paper can't do it alone. The understanding and commitment of top management and the translation of this understanding and commitment to everyone in the organization is required. It may not be easy to achieve, but whatever effort is expended is well worth it.

SELECTED EXERCISES

1. Place a phone call to your company. Count the number of rings before someone answers. If you can do so anonymously (if you can't, call another company), pose as a prospect or vendor. Make a mental note as to how the person answering the phone handles your call.

2. Call your biggest competitor. Do the same as in #1 above. Hopefully, for your sake, your company will perform better.

3. Examine your company's Policy and Procedures manual (if your company has one) along with the other documents referred to above in this Chapter (queries to solicit customer's satisfaction with your service, pieces used to thank customers, case histories/testimonials, customer birthday cards, etc.). In your opinion, do they effectively promote positive word-of-mouth advertising.

4. Audit the attitude and commitment of your top management and employees to taking care of customers. Does this promote positive word-of-mouth advertising.

5. Do you have a form upon which marketing information (complaints, compliments, etc.) can be collected from customers and reported to marketing? If so, is it adequate? If not, redesign it using the *Market Information Form* of Figure 15-1 as a guide.

Chapter 16 • OTHER MARKETING PIECES

"There are many ways to get from A to B..."

The marketing vehicles discussed so far are those that are commonly used by most companies. There are many others which may or may not be employed as part of your company's promotional mix. Their inclusion in the "other" category doesn't necessarily mean that they are any less important than the other marketing examples already discussed. For certain companies and products, they may even prove to be more important. They are included in the other category for a variety of reasons including: they may be new and less well-known; expensive and out of the reach of most organizations; involve the same creation techniques as previously discussed marketing pieces; inaccessible to all companies; or unproven.

SALES PROMOTIONS.

Sales promotions are "special offers" aimed at getting the prospects to buy now. They often involve a discount, a giveaway, a bonus, or some other incentive for acting right away. They are very effective at prompting buyers of products to purchase now. One would assume that they are not so effective at encouraging buyers of higher-priced non-commodity high-tech products to move any faster. This is not always true. If executed properly, they can work for any product.

Types of Sales Promotions

There are many different kinds of Sales Promotions. The following is a representative list:

Discounts: A reduction in price is offered if the prospect orders within a certain period.

Bonuses: Bonuses (usually in the form of options, accessories, upgrades, and/or supplies) are included at no additional charge if the prospect purchases by a certain date.

Giveaways: An item such as a coffee mug, pen and pencil set, flashlight, or some other inexpensive item is offered if a purchase is made within a definite time period. These "Specialty Advertising" items, as they are called, typically have the name, address and phone number of the company on them.

Coupons: A free booklet, manual, training course, or some other product-related item is offered if a prospect sends in a coupon from an advertisement. Coupons are a good way of measuring the effectiveness of an ad.

Gift Certificates: Gift certificates often attract prospects who want to give gifts to friends and relatives, but who want to let the recipient decide. They are a form of sales promotion particularly since recipients have to take some sort of buying action in response to receiving them. Furthermore, many pre-paid certificates reflect discounts or cost less than the face value of the certificate. The airlines have started selling special discounted certificates and coupon books to flyers who meet certain qualifications.

Sales Promotion Do's

Care and Taste. In professional and high-tech industries, sales promotions should be conducted with great care and taste. The company should avoid any sales promotions that might appear to be cheap, low-class, or in bad taste. The sales promotions must be in harmony with the company's positioning strategies.

Have a Good Reason For Doing. There should be a good reason for doing a sales promotion, and this reason should be communicated clearly to prospects and customers. Good reasons include: inventory clearance, seasonal clearance, holiday special, seminar special, show special, special occasion, new product introduction, old product clearance, end-of-year or end-of-quarter special (to meet sales quotas or lower inventory taxes).

Assign a Time Limit. Most sales promotions should have a definite time limit associated with them. If not, the discounted price will become the new de facto price, and the company will never be able to go back to the original suggested list price. If sales promotions prove to be very successful, they can always be extended. The reason for the extension should be clearly communicated to prospects and customers. For example, such reasons as "Due to the heavy demand..."; "Because many customers didn't receive notice of the discount..."; and "Since we still have a couple of older models remaining..." are typical reasons for extending promotion deadlines.
Don'ts

Sales promotion "don'ts"

Don't do anything to cheapen product or the company. A misguided sales promotion can undo a good position and hurt the image of the product and company. Any promotional ideas should be reviewed by several senior marketing and sales personnel before they are implemented.

Don't insult the intelligence of your publics. Many promotions are really insulting. They treat intelligent adults as if they were mindless morons. This won't work with high-tech products. High-tech products are serious and require intelligence to operate. Promotions should be in line with this position.

YELLOW PAGES.

While the Yellow Pages also address a rather general audience, this form of advertising has proven to be very effective for all commodity-type products. The reasons for this include: a Yellow Pages listing has a life of at least one year; prospects who look in the Yellow Pages are usually ready to buy the product; and small companies can appear as large as big companies through their trademark ads in the Yellow Pages.

In recent years, the Yellow Pages have become more sophisticated in the options that are offered. A listing can be in special consumer, business, or neighborhood directories. There are regular listings, boldface listings, listings in red, trademark listings, or display ads. Although many directory sales people claim a display ad is the most effective, some studies show that the trademark listing can be just as effective for a lot less money. The trademark listing stands out because it puts your logo, address, phone number and/or slogan in place of the regular listing. Because it appears alphabetically in the column where your regular listing would be, it can be more easily found than a display ad, which is sometimes out of sequence on a different page. Also, since all trademark ads are the same size, a smaller company can appear as large the largest company.

The process of creating a display ad is basically the same as any print ad so it won't be repeated here. In fact, many companies merely re-format their print ads to conform to the mechanical requirements of the particular directory when placing a display ad in the Yellow Pages.

There are now many different Yellow Pages directories from different companies. All of them tell you that theirs is the best. You should go with the one that gives you the best coverage. While it would be inappropriate to endorse one over another, studies show that the one which is distributed by your main phone company is the one which is most widely used. Depending on the degree of coverage overlap, you might consider advertising in more than one directory. You never know which one a "hot" prospect might look in first.

INDUSTRY DIRECTORIES.

Industry specific directories are particularly good sources for advertising high-tech products. The reasons include: they are typically inexpensive, they cover specific market niches, and they usually have a life of at least one year. They are most useful in those industries in which they are used frequently. For example, The Parker Directory is used daily by people in the California legal community because it lists all the names, addresses and phone numbers of courts, practicing judges and lawyers throughout the state. The Writers Guild Directory is a frequently-used directory in the entertainment industry. If one of your target market industries uses such a directory frequently, you should seriously consider advertising in that directory. At the very least, you should familiarize yourself with the various industry directories your target markets use regularly. You should keep these on file in the company's marketing library for future consideration.

As with the Yellow Pages, the process of creating ads in industry directories is the same as any other print ads.

COMPUTER BULLETIN BOARDS.

A new kind of advertising has developed along with the personal computer. It is the computer bulletin board. In most cases, this type of advertising is free (other than the cost of the program and the computer access time). Using a bulletin board program, all an advertiser has to do is put up a message on the computer screen. Any users who have access to this bulletin board have access to the message. This has proven to be a particularly effective way of communicating with high-tech prospects since many are computer literate and use bulletin boards often. A customer of a computer seminar company wanted to let his colleagues know of a seminar he thought they'd like to attend. He put a description of the seminar on the company's computer bulletin board. The reaction was phenomenal. A large number of interested colleagues signed up for the $1,100 per person seminar much to the delight of the seminar company. In response, the seminar company looked for situations in which it could put ads on other company billboards. In another example, Phil DeGuere, the executive producer and head writer of the former hit TV Show "Simon and Simon" used a computer billboard program to sample and create interest in the show when it was a new and fledgling production. Due to the impressive response of computer billboard users, CBS was persuaded to keep the show. Subsequently, it went on to become a hit for several years.

Depending on the purpose of the ad, creating a billboard ad can follow the same processes as creating directory listings, invitations to seminars, or personal direct mail letters.

ELECTRONIC MAIL.

Similar to billboards, Electronic Mail can send messages over a computer network to all or selected users of the network. For similar reasons, this can be an effective form of marketing if properly and discreetly used. It is best used to stay in contact with market targets who already know you. If used to create new business, extra care must be taken to insure that your e-mail is not thought of as "junk" e-mail.

FAX MACHINES.

With the rapid spread of FAX machines in the office, a new type of advertising is being employed. An advertiser's FAX system can be programmed to dial up and transmit complete ads to the FAX machines of selected market targets. While this can be effective, it can anger prospects if it is not used discreetly and with their prior permission. As with electronic mail, many prospects don't want their systems tied up with advertisements — particularly if they are using them to complete their own work under deadline pressures. Before using this promotional method, it is recommended that prospects be contacted to obtain their permission before sending them promotional material.

As with billboards and electronic mail advertising, the FAX machine is a delivery system more than a type of marketing piece. Therefore, virtually any type of print marketing (from personal letter to sophisticated print ad) can be transmitted by this system. You should understand that the quality received on the other end is largely outside your control since the paper and print quality depends on the FAX machine that market targets have in their offices.

VIDEO TAPE.

Although most TV ads are done on video tape, the video tape in this section refers to another form of marketing whereby the ad is distributed to the consumer in the form of a video tape (rather than a TV broadcast). It involves creating a sort of mini movie that is longer and therefore more able to detail the features of a product than a 30-second TV spot. Car manufacturers, travel companies, and various high-tech companies who can benefit from showing their products under actual operating conditions are finding success using this marketing vehicle. In fact, some of these companies have even been successful selling their videos to cover their production costs. Isuzu has been selling a videotape showing a stunt driver and his female boss who fall in love with their Isuzus and each other for $9.95. When you think about it, spending $10 for a video tape which details the operation of a product under "actual" operating conditions is probably more informative and less expensive (in terms of time, gas, and other inconveniences) than visiting dealer showrooms.

The process of creating a video tape piece is virtually the same as creating a lengthy TV commercial. There are production and various post-production costs (editing, special effects, audio sweetening, etc.). Depending on the format and the quality, these costs can vary substantially. The average TV commercial cost over $147,000 to produce in 1987. The Isuzu video cost $150,000 to produce.

CABLE TV.

With all of the cable TV channels and the ability to focus on specific groups of prospects, cable TV holds promise as an effective source of advertising products to all types of niche markets. Many large companies even have their own networks. You should find out the extent to which your prospects view cable TV and evaluate this potential source accordingly. The production of a cable TV ad follows much the same process as the creation of a broadcast TV ad, unless of course the ad is delivered live in which case you don't have to pay exorbitant production costs (which averaged over $147,000 per TV ad in 1987 and over $150,000 in the outset of the 90's).

OUTDOOR ADVERTISING.

Billboards, bus-stop shelters and benches, busses and taxi-cabs can be effective vehicles for advertising. Because this type of advertising reaches a very general audience it is best-suited for consumer products that have a very broad audience. The creation of outdoor ads involves much the same process as print media ads. The main difference is that the motion of the ad relative to the consumer must be considered when designing the ad. The impact of this motion is that the headline and picture become even more important. Since the ad is moving relative to the reader, there shouldn't be a lot of text since the non-pedestrian readers don't have time to read more than a couple of lines.

Since outdoor advertising space is a specialized market, there aren't as many media selection choices as there are with other types of ads.

ELECTRONIC SHOPPING.

As mentioned previously, electronic shopping networks have become a popular way of advertising and distributing certain consumer products. They have potential with certain high-tech commodity products since the buyer can view the product as well as receive a detailed description. However, more expensive and complex high-tech products are not likely to be effectively promoted by this method. The price and the complexity of such products usually dictates the need for several face-to-face meetings between the sales person and the prospect. Also, most purchasers' work schedules are incompatible with the time slots of electronic shopping programs. In the future, with the advent of interactive television, electronic shopping might prove to be a more effective high-tech advertising vehicle.

NETWORKING.

Networking is a term borrowed from the electronics and computer fields which has crept into the business vocabulary during the 1980s. Analogous to word-of-mouth advertising, networking refers to activities designed for people to meet, form business relationships and refer business to each other.

While it may be new to the business vocabulary, the concept is not new. It is really an old form of promotion embodied in the many clubs and associations that have formed over many years. The Chamber of Commerce, Kiwanis Club, Optimists Club, Friars Club, the American Marketing Association, and various other groups are really organizations for networking. The idea is that it is preferable to do business with people you know and trust than people you don't know — particularly if those people will also refer business to you in return.

Joining clubs and groups can be a very effective way of helping to market a company and its products. In addition to the contacts made in these organizations, members have opportunities to speak to their local chapters as well as to regional and national chapters. Whenever speakers are introduced, their company affiliations are usually mentioned. This is an effective means of spreading the company name to a large number of people. Also, high-level leads and ideas are often generated during these networking activities. That's why it's usually a good idea for marketing and sales personnel to participate — especially in those organizations which have a significant number of people from the company's target market segments.

The marketing pieces used in the process of actively creating networking opportunities include the following: sending out letters to key organizations and clubs to get key personnel included on invitation and mailing lists; creating effective business cards; and inviting influential people from important organizations to important company functions and seminars.

PROPOSALS.

An important promotional tool for many companies — especially those doing business in the public sector — is the proposal. The proposal is prepared to describe how the company and its products will meet the specific needs of a prospect. These needs are often specified in an RFP (Request for Proposal), SBIR (Small Business Innovative Research) Program Solicitation Manual, and/or various other public and private sector publications.

Although the proposal is a unique promotional tool, it employs basically the same marketing strategies, principles and techniques as other forms of promotion. The proposal should:

Be Responsive to Needs

As with any form of promotion, the proposal must be responsive to the needs of the prospect. These needs are usually very clearly delineated in the RFP or solicitation manual. Therefore, to insure success, the proposal should respond to every detail in the solicitation request. If, for some reason, the company and its products cannot fulfill a particular detail of the specification, the proposal should positively explain how it would satisfy the need in perhaps a different way rather than ignore, or "slide over" the point.

Employ Advertising Techniques

The guidelines presented in the section on the UMS apply to proposals as well. A proposal should be attractive and make it easy for the reader to pick out the important points without having to reread the entire document. It should clearly position the company and its products to differentiate it from the competition. It should be concise, clear, and to the point. Since the reader is going to have to read many proposals, the proposal should be designed to make the reading task as easy on the reader as possible — i.e. by employing, lots of space, an easy-to-read type font, and pictures and graphs where appropriate.

Stress Cost, or Return on Investment, over Price

Both private and public sector organizations often use the RFP as means to get the bid price of the product(s) being solicited as low as possible. As a result, price is usually a very important part of a proposal's marketing strategy. In anticipation that other bids may be lower, the company should stress that its alternative is the "lowest cost" alternative, and it should explain the difference between cost and price. How can a company be the lowest cost alternative when it isn't the lowest price? There is usually a simple explanation. A company may have designed its product so that it costs less to operate and fix than other alternatives; it may include support and service in its quoted price which effectively lowers the cost of the product; and it may warranty the product over a longer period which lowers maintenance and service costs.

In addition to stressing the difference between *cost* and *price, it is also useful to explain how, no matter what the price,* its solution will yield the greatest return on investment. That is, while other alternatives may be priced lower, they are also likely to yield a lower return.

Consider Greater Marketing Objectives

The company should look upon the proposal as a promotional tool whose objectives go beyond that of winning just one project award. Even if the company is not selected, the good impression made by its proposal may have impact on the award of the next project. Furthermore, a well-done proposal will be better remembered, will most-likely be kept on file for a long time, and will go a long way toward developing a good relationship with the soliciting organization. If nothing else, it will contribute toward a positive image of the company.

POINT OF SALE DISPLAYS.

Point of sale displays are freestanding floor or table displays which are designed to promote a product or family of products. In some cases, they are created by enlarging ads and mounting them on self-standing structures made of cardboard or other supporting materials. In other cases, they are designed to actually hold samples of the product. Depending on the purpose for which it will be used, the display can take a variety of different two or three-dimensional shapes and forms. The process of creating the advertising part of the display is much the same as creating any print ad. As for the functional part of the display, the structure has be constructed to easily fit in with its intended use. It should be large enough to attract sufficient foot traffic, but small and lightweight enough to fit into most of the already-crowded retail spaces.

PACKAGING.

In addition to having the main function of protecting the product during shipping, packaging is an important part of the promotional strategy. Often it is the first item that buyers see when the product is delivered. Also, the packaging of many non-perishable usually has a long shelf life. It will sit on shelves of distributors and dealers before it is sold; it will pass through normal shipping channels and make impressions on everyone involved along the way; it will often be kept by customers in the event that the product has to be shipped to another location or back to the manufacturer; and some will even use it to carry belongings when moving. As a result, packaging should be as attractive as possible, have the company and product logos prominently displayed, and should display any good slogans or awards won by the product.

With certain consumer-oriented high-tech products, the company will pay more for packaging than for producing the product. Even in the more typical case where the package consists of a cardboard box, the company should consider the box as a vehicle for "free" advertising. It affords the company another opportunity to convince the customer that he/she has made the right decision.

BOOKS, MANUALS, AND PRODUCT INSTRUCTIONS.

While more typically identified as part of the product, books, manuals, and product instructions are also important promotional vehicles. Before purchasing certain products, some prospective buyers will ask to see associated books, manuals, and product instructions. The impression made by these can either help or hinder the sale. Help is obviously what it should do.

Some companies, such as Digital Equipment Corporation (affectionately know by the acronym DEC) believe in providing books or booklets as part of their marketing strategy. These books usually offer product details about entire product lines or focus on products for specific target industries.

Similar principles which apply to the company's marketing literature should apply to this product literature. In technical markets, product literature is often a main vehicle for promoting sales of the product.

THE INTERNET, WORLD WIDE WEB, AND ON-LINE MARKETING.

Perhaps the fastest growing method of promoting companies and products is via the Internet. In fact, the Internet is becoming such an important marketing vehicle that devoting an entire chapter in this book would not do it justice. Perhaps the greatest aspect of the Internet is that any company, no matter how small, can reach a worldwide market effectively, via the Internet. The reason is that once you create a Web site, list your site with various portals and search engines, and promote your site by advertising it in both conventional and new ways, people looking for what you are selling can find you or stumble upon you no matter where they are located in the world.

The flip side of the enormous opportunities provided by the Internet are equally large traps. Perhaps the biggest trap is that too many marketers have failed to realize that the Internet is a powerful tool — not an end-all objective. That is, they need to understand the capabilities and limitations of the tool and use it accordingly. Moreover, they need to remember the basic fundamentals of marketing and communications. Early Web developers fell in love with the complex graphics and animations possible on the Internet. They forgot about the most important element in any marketing equation — the buyer. Shoppers want to get information quickly without waiting for it. Once they get the information they need, they want to buy just as quickly and easily. Too many Web sites flood the senses of visitors with complex and confusing graphics. Even worse, while they are being confused, these visitors have to wait for complex graphics and animations to download on their computers. This is such a pervasive problem that to many "www" doesn't stand for World Wide Web, it represents World Wide Wait. To make most effective use of the Internet, learn about its limitations as well as its opportunities. Then use the tool to optimal advantage.

THE OTHER "OTHER" MARKETING PIECES.

There are many other marketing vehicles which can be employed to promote a company's products. They are mentioned here to remind you that, no matter how exhaustive your marketing program or your creative ideas, there are always additional approaches you can try. They include such methods as skywriting, distribution of leaflets, ad space on the face of airline tickets, door-to-door solicitation (Avon and Fuller Brush), visible product labels, T-shirt ad messages, and physical bulletin boards wherever they may be located. Can you think of others? The list is virtually infinite — limited only by the bounds of your imagination.

SELECTED EXERCISES.

1. From the marketing vehicles described in this chapter, select those which you believe would be appropriate for your organization. Try to rank them according to their importance to your company.
2. Develop the requisite marketing pieces for each of the top three on your list.

Chapter 17 • CONCLUSION

"All good things must come to an end..."

I hope you feel that this book has achieved its stated purpose — to help you create much of your own marketing so that you can be more self-reliant and more effective without increasing your marketing budget. While you probably will continue to use outside professionals to put the finishing touches on some of your most important ads and brochures, you can save considerable time and money and retain control over your marketing projects by doing most of the groundwork yourself. Additionally, for many of your marketing pieces which don't require magazine or brochure quality, you can do them completely yourself.

Rather than summarize the entire book, it makes more sense to leave you with the most important concepts to remember when creating your own marketing pieces.

EVERYTHING IS CONNECTED.

No marketing piece should be done in isolation. It should fit in with what has come before and what will come after. What has come before includes, in hierarchical order, the company's organization structure, business plan, the marketing plan, promotional strategies, and objectives of the particular marketing piece to be created. What will come after includes the distribution of the piece, measurement of its effectiveness, reporting results to management, revisions based on feedback received, and a repeat of the whole cycle on the next iteration. The problem with much of the marketing created by organizations and their ad agencies is that they look at each piece as an isolated project. This kind of thinking can lead to serious problems. When creating a marketing piece, make sure you

know and think about what has come before and what will come
after.

FUNDAMENTALS.

To create effective marketing, you have to understand and use
marketing fundamentals. All marketing pieces should incorporate image, the appropriate mix of (one or more of) the 5 Ps, and
a mechanism for measuring the effectiveness of the piece and
taking corrective action.

UNIVERSAL MARKETING STRUCTURE.

Virtually all effective marketing pieces use a structure which I
call the Universal Marketing Structure, or the UMS. In its
complete form, it consists of the headline, body text, format,
photo, close, and signature. The headline is the most important
since many more people read the headline than read the other
portions of a marketing piece. By understanding the UMS and
by following it to properly communicate the main message(s) of
the marketing piece, you can create more effective marketing.

NON-LINEARITY OF SPACE AND TIME.

Most people find it very difficult to really understand marketing.
Many even think it is magic, and don't care to know how it
works. The reason for this is that there are certain psychological aspects of marketing which are more difficult to quantify.
One of these is the non-linearity of space and time. Some
marketing pieces, which are very long, are a joy to read and
seem to be brief. Others are quite short, but seem very tedious
and long. Some examples of marketing have few words, but
appear to be crowded. Others have many words, but don't seem
crowded at all. The reason is the non-linearity of space and
time. If you create pieces that are fun to read and that are
graphically balanced, you will use this non-linearity to your
advantage in reaching your market targets.

HOOKS, LINES AND SINKERS.

Because most people are "numb" from their exposure to an estimated 20,000 ad messages per week, you need to create marketing pieces with strong "hooks" to grab their attention and to get them to remember your main message. Since most people are very busy and many are also lazy, they don't have the time or interest to read many of the marketing pieces to which they are exposed. Because they typically have to read the headline just to make the determination whether or not to continue reading the rest of an ad, the hook is best placed in the headline, as is the main message. In fact, in many cases, the entire headline becomes the hook. Those pieces which don't have strong hooks are doomed to sink into oblivion.

PERSONAL RELATIONSHIPS.

Marketing is much more effective when it succeeds in building a personal rapport or relationship with prospective buyers. People buy from people and/or companies which they trust and with which they are comfortable. By thinking of your marketing as "making new friendships" while enhancing old ones, you are likely to be several steps ahead of your competition.

NO NEGATIVES.

In creating effective marketing, negatives should be avoided. While they are used in many ads, the most effective ones avoid them because they don't want to alienate any portions of the potential buying audience.

TELL THE TRUTH.

Few people want to develop relationships with liars. Therefore, your marketing should always tell the truth. If it doesn't, it can erode the trust between you and your publics and damage your relationship with them. In addition to telling the truth, the truth should be believable. If it's not believed, the effect is the same as if you have told a lie.

ANSWER OBJECTIONS.

In order to sell their products, all companies have to answer customer and prospect objections. Marketing pieces are an excellent vehicle for doing this. Rather than "sweep these objections under the rug", your marketing should confront them directly and answer them honestly in such a way as to emphasize the benefits and advantages of your products.

TURN NEGATIVES INTO POSITIVES.

Most companies receive some negative publicity or incur public relations damage at some point during their lifetime. When these negatives occur, you should look at them as an opportunity to do something extra for your publics so that you are viewed as a "hero". In this way, you turn the negatives into positives which work in your favor. A simple example of this occurs when your company does something to make one of your customers angry. Rather than make excuses, you can turn the anger into an advantage by simply apologizing and sending the customer flowers.

BE UNIQUE.

As the late Rosser Reeves espoused in his Unique Selling Principle, all marketing pieces should sell something, and that something should be unique to your company and/or products. It should differentiate your products from the competition. Otherwise, why should they buy from you?

PROMPT A BUYING ACTION.

All marketing pieces should be designed to prompt a buying action on the part of your market targets. If not a sale, this buying action might be to complete and send in a coupon for more information; come in for a demonstration; pick up a free gift or catalog; or schedule an appointment to discuss your needs.

BE ON TARGET.

Effective marketing pieces are aimed at the target audience. Since many more people read the headline than the other parts of the piece, it's a good idea to identify the target(s) in the headline. If this is not possible, the picture or graphic or the highlighted subheads are the next best choices.

EVERYTHING WORTH REPEATING SHOULD BE REPEATED.

For marketing to be effective, it has to be repeated. The reasons include the following:

- **Coverage.** Some targets don't get to read all issues or receive all mailings. If you advertise once or twice, they may miss your ad.

- **Timing and the moving *Buying Window*.** Some of your targets may not be in the market when the see the first few ads, but are in the market when they see a subsequent ad which reminds them of your product.

- **Cumulative Effect.** Advertising is cumulative. Since most targets are so saturated with messages, they tune yours out during the first few runs. After seeing your name over and over, it begins to penetrate the thick barriers which they built up.

- **Out of sight... Out of mind.** If you advertise only once or twice, many prospects will think you went out of business which is not good for your image or your sales. Others will just forget you because you are not there to compete with all the others who are.

CUSTOMER SATISFACTION.

The ultimate goal of marketing is to create customer satisfaction, which, in turn, will generate more sales and create a *positive word-of-mouth pyramid.* To achieve this goal, you should think of the audience throughout the creation cycle. If you do, you will make the piece informative, easy to read, easy to understand, and believable. The result of your success will be more buying actions and more sales.

FINAL COMMENTS.

This concludes the subject matter of this book. I hope that you have learned something of value from your reading, and I wish you much success in applying the concepts and techniques to your marketing. If nothing else, you should feel more comfortable about creating your own marketing pieces or reviewing the work of others whom you hire to do them for you. You have the talent. If, for some reason, you lack the confidence, you can overcome this difficulty with practice. The best way to learn is by doing. To help you, there is one last set of exercises below. Good luck!

FINAL EXERCISES.

1. Create the marketing pieces you need for your organization.

2. Follow the concepts and techniques discussed in this book.

3. Write to us at K&A Press to let us know how well they worked. Also, let us know if something didn't work, and give us your reasons why.

4. If possible, send us examples of the work you've created.

5. Keep thinking that you can create whatever marketing you want to create. If you don't think this way, you will limit yourself needlessly.

REFERENCES

Alsop, Ronald and Abrams, Bill (ed.), *The Wall Street Journal on Marketing*, New York: Dow Jones-Irwin, 1986.

Bayan, Richard, *Words That Sell*, Chicago and New York: Contemporary Books, 1984.

Bovée, Courtland L. and Arens, William F., *Contemporary Advertising*, Homewood, IL: Irwin, 1992.

Buzzell, Robert D. (ed.), *Marketing in an Electronic Age*, Boston: The Harvard Business School Press, 1985.

Demoney, Jerry and Meyer, Susan E., *Pasteups & Mechanicals*, New York: Watson-Guptil Publications, 1982.

Kalb, Ira S., *High-tech Marketing: A Practical Approach*, Los Angeles: K&A Press, 1988 and 1992.

Kalb, Ira S., *Selling High-tech Products and Services*, Los Angeles: K&A Press, 1991.

Kalb, Ira S., *Structuring Your Business For Success*, Los Angeles: K&A Press, 1993.

Kalb, Ira S., *Marketing Your Legal Services*, Los Angeles: K&A Press, 1993.

Munce, Howard, *Graphics Handbook*, Cincinnati: North Light Publishers, 1982.

Ries, Al and Trout Jack, *Positioning: The Battle for Your Mind*, New York: Warner Books, 1986.

Notes.

Index